Shaping My Identity

Shaping My Identity

@2026 Gwenette Cambridge

Published by Hobo Jungle Press
St. Vincent & the Grenadines, W.I.
Sharon, Connecticut, USA

First edition
May 2026

Printed in the United States of America

ISBN #978-976-97664-5-7
Library of Congress Control Number: 202693728

Shaping My Identity

Through the Eyes of a Child

Gwenette Pearson Cambridge

Illustrated by Christine Browne

"Childhood memories are the sweetest treats."

Author Unknown

"It takes courage to grow up and become
who you really are!"

E. E. Cummings

Contents

Colloquial Expressions

Taste her hand—To partake of food that a person cooked to determine whether it was tasty or not.

Flattie of rum— The shape of the rum bottle was like a flat flask.

Metemgee—a mixture of provisions cooked in coconut milk and served with fried or steamed fish and fluffy dumplings.

Pork-knockers—A term used in Guyana and Suriname to describe small-scale gold miners who work in the interior or remote areas in Guyana. The name may have originated from their diet of pickled or cured pork.

Broddough—A name is given to someone who receives clothes from other people who live abroad or are good financial standing. Such persons no longer want the clothes and give them away.

Goat-mouth—A person is said to have 'goat-mouth' if a bad thing they predicted for another person comes true.

Comess—Gossip

Not quite right in the head—A person who is regarded as mad or crazy

Dixing English voice—To imitate the accent spoken in another country

Trust meh—A colloquial expression used for "credit"

Prologue

Memories are like a tidal swirl of leaves after a heavy wind storm. They rise to the surface of my mind like wispy clouds seeking to find a cluster. The mellow evening sun bathes the flat landscape of Golden Grove village located on the eastern side of the coastal plain of Guyana. I sit in the rocking chair strategically placed so I can see all those who pass by and peer across the road to the house where Miss Verda had once lived. It is now an old, abandoned building. Tall trees obscure the windows and clumps of grass sneak in around the foundation. The grass looks back at the trees as though a conversation is taking place. On the radio "Memories Don't Leave Like People Do" by Johnny Bristol is playing. This song is a fitting reflection of what I feel as memories crowd my mind. I ignore the wrinkles and veins that run beneath my translucent skin and see instead a young girl full of vigour and brimming with life. Was it fifty or sixty years ago? I can't remember because the years have passed by so swiftly. However, I distinctly recall the men and women who helped to shape my identity and taught me the values of tolerance and compassion. I recall those childhood friends as well who impacted my life. The memories emerge in my mind one by one, like actors awaiting their cues to come on stage and act out their roles.

Chapter One

Back Then

My name is Sumitra Gallenger, but everyone calls me Sue (my family only called me Sumitra when I misbehaved). When I was a little girl, I lived with Granny Shiela in the village of Triumph. My mother, Dorothy, left for Curaçao after she became pregnant by a married man—not her husband. The scandal nearly brought Granny Shiela to her knees after the adulterer's wife alerted the entire village about Dorothy being a "husband stealer" and a "home breaker". According to Granny Shiela, my mother, Dorothy, had a new life in Curaçao with a husband and five children.

Auntie Gillie, Granny Shiela's youngest daughter, and her husband, Tom, lived with us. They had no children of their own, but because I had joined the family when I was little, they often mentioned (within my hearing) that they would adopt me as their own daughter. It never mattered to me since I never knew my mother. This was the only life I knew.

Uncle Tom worked at the main office of brewery about eight miles from Georgetown in a village called Beterverwagting on the east coast of Guyana. He preferred to work in Thirst Park on the outskirts of Georgetown since the men who worked there benefited more than those in the countryside. For instance, those in town were more likely to get bottles of beers at a reduced price or for free. However, Uncle Tom could only get the watchman job in the country area.

My cousin Alicia, who was six years older than me, also lived with us. When she was little, her father, Granny Shiela's only son, brought her to visit during the summer holidays. Years later, I heard Auntie Gillie saying, "Creighton was spoilt because he was the only boy in the family." One year when he brought Alicia for summer, he never looked back. He was always "in his cups," Granny Shiela said. He never gave Granny Shiela any financial support for Alicia and eventually she stopped looking.

Alicia was a sulky child who looked as though she carried the entire world on her shoulders. She mostly kept to herself and only spoke if she had to. On the other hand, I called out to everyone who passed our house. I would pay close attention when the older people chatted, soaking in every bit of their conversations. Uncle Tom told Auntie Gillie my ears were "light, that I had a phenomenal memory and would go far in life.

In the days before computers, people relied heavily on "brain power." We ate a variety of foods that nourished the brain. A person whose brain was weak, according to our elders, was bound to fail at everything. Therefore, we gorged on eggnogs, fish, or the roe of the fish, as well as greens, greens and more greens! Dishes, such as carilla, known as bitter melon in some parts of the world, were cooked regularly with saltfish or minced meat in coconut milk to enrich their taste, while at the same time it was expected to get rid of toxins in the blood or other illnesses associated with diabetes.

When I was four years old, we moved from the village of Triumph to Golden Grove. I was sad about the disruption of my familiar place of abode, but I was snug and warm in the horse cart carrying us to our new home. I remember the cart rocking rhythmically, the pots and pans clanking and rattling in the back of the cart. Fireflies flickered like fairy lights in the blackness of the night. The only other light was the flambeau, a jug consisting of a piece of cloth forced down into a jar of kerosene oil and held aloft in the hand of the man who drove the horse cart. The flambeau was not so much for the driver, who traversed the road four to six times a day and knew the road like the back of his hand, but for the new "horseless" vehicles that were ever so slowly replacing the horse carts. The sudden blare of a car horn could spook the horse, and it would ignore the reins of the driver and gallop to safety, wherever it could be found.

At first Golden Grove seemed a lot like Triumph. Men still sat on their donkeys to discuss who should have won the last cricket match and the sound of horses clip-clopping on their way to market was a regular occurrence. Women with big baskets of vegetables on their heads called out to villagers, their voices rising and falling rhythmically, "Any ochroes, bora or cucumbers fuh yuh neighba?"

Since most of the villages in Guyana are located on the coast, which is close to 300 miles long, we enjoyed the soothing breeze from the Atlantic Ocean. Just outside the village was a big playing field. We went there whenever we wanted to run to get rid of our excess energy.

Three roads ran parallel to each other, with houses leaning haphazardly in different directions. Babies appeared regularly on the hips of women who wore voluminous dresses and straw hats to protect their faces from the scorching sun. A neighbour often popped into our yard to borrow some salt or sugar, cooking oil or even a pot to boil water. Back then, it was an unspoken rule that what was borrowed was never returned.

Privacy didn't exist in Golden Grove. Everybody's business was like an open book, and secrets shared privately were broadcast publicly in the market square wherever a group of women huddled together. It was generally accepted that several outbursts with expletives hurled like flaming swords between neighbours who felt their trust had been violated or someone had "bad-mouthed" them behind their backs. When there was a death in the family or at the birth of a baby, though, all was forgiven. Quarrels were forgotten like discarded garbage, and everyone became friends again.

I found joy in running naked in the rain or playing in the mud. "Sue Gallenger," my auntie would say giving me a little shake, "When yuh ketch a cold and get sick who would have to stay up to look after yuh?" Then she bundled me inside for a bath and a cup of Quaker oats porridge.

Animals were treated like family members, (we had a small poodle called Chooloo because it would chew up our slippers in the porch) and a communal pot was organized at month end when husbands or the "chile father" got paid. A big pot of meat bubbling on the fire tantalized my nostrils but we waited patiently because we knew everyone would get a taste of the delicious meal. The words "violence and murder" were unheard of, and village life was like a magic brew of never-ending happiness. This enchanted bubble characterised village life. But one day, it all changed when I noticed the strange faces appearing in what I considered 'my village.'

Guided Questions

1. What is the name of the main character of this story?
2. Where is the story mainly set? From which village did the main character travel?
3. Compare the settings of the two villages.
4. What is the major theme in this chapter?
5. The writer compares two stages in her life. What are those stages?
6. Give an example of onomatopoeia used in this chapter.
7. Examine the use of the term "exhaustive illness". What does this mean?
8. Find a word or phrase that can be used to describe "magic brew".

Discussion

The writer mentions one stage of village life that might be different from your way of life. Discuss this way of life.

What are some of the things parents give children today to make them grow strong and healthy?

One of the writer's childhood experiences was being given carilla to get "rid of toxins". What practices can you remember your parents or grandparents engaging in to ensure your body stayed healthy?

Mention has been made of a place called "Beterverwagting". This is a Dutch name for the country that helped to colonize Guyana. Are there any areas in your country associated with names of countries that once occupied your lands?

Why do you think people from the smaller Caribbean islands went to live in Curaçao?

Chapter Two

The Changing Face of the Village

As I grew older I realized that change was inevitable. I saw this reflected in my village. Dirt tracks metamorphosed into paved roads and new houses appeared regularly like a ding-dong of clock chiming at twelve each day or night. The village population increased with the arrival of Mr. Sobers, an army veteran who had been honourably discharged (whatever that meant) from the British army. He lived in Pike Street.

Some days as I passed by the Sobers' house, holding tightly to Auntie Gillie's hand, I would notice Mrs. Sobers swinging idly in her hammock with a cigarette in one hand and a cup of tea in the other. I couldn't stop staring at her blonde hair; Auntie Gillie said she had blue eyes. She smiled without moving her lips and her words were clipped and brief. According to Miss Daisie, the clarion gossiper of the villager, "Ah cyant understand hide or hair of wha she say."

Unlike the wooden shacks covered with sheets of galvanize nailed askew, Mr. Sobers' house was made of mahogany, gleaming like polished brown berries in the sunlight. A garage was attached to house Mr. Sobers' vehicle—a Bentley that came all the way from England. At first, we were all fascinated by the shiny car as well as the family who lived there, but our interest in the Sobers' family soon waned and they were allowed to live in peace.

Soon after the arrival of Mr. Sobers, Mr. Hardat came with his wife and two teenage sons. He was an Indian man who wore his Punjabi with pride and his turban with dignity. He opened a grocery shop that sold everything under the sun—from kerosene oil to salted butter; but most importantly, he offered credit to the villagers!

My Granny Shiela sniffed, "I not going there to credit anything. People must learn to be content with the little they have. The Bible say, 'little is much when God is in it'." I was accustomed to my granny's sayings even though I could not understand what she meant. However, on one or two occasions Granny Shiela visited Mr. Hardat's shop when she ran out of some grocery items. Of course I went with her!

Mr. Hardat lived in the apartment above the shop, but most nights he slept in a room to the back of the shop in case someone tried to break in and steal his goods. An attempted burglary at the start of Mr. Hardat's business made him more vigilant about his business operation. He certainly wasn't taking any chances.

Mrs. Hardat was a quiet Indian woman draped from head to toe in her silk sari, a red dot in the middle of her forehead advertising her married status. Her gold bangles jingled as she handed the grocery over the counter. Her sons did the weighing and packing.

Mr. Hardat kept a record of everyone who asked for credit whether it was half a pound of lard or three ounces of cheese. He carefully wrote he names of the creditors with a black ink pen in a hard cover notebook he kept upstairs in his house. I admired the way he could remember who owed him or how much without referring to the book.

To avoid having a crowded shop, Mr. Hardat asked people to pre-order their groceries by sending in their list early. He clipped the list on a string, and they would flutter in the scant, but welcoming breeze in the airless room.

Mr. Hardat's credit system affected the way the villagers related to one another. No longer did neighbours borrow salt, or rice or sugar from each other, but sent for credit at Mr. Hardat's grocery store. Neighbours became spiteful, especially when they saw the children coming with heavy bags from Mr. Hardat's shop.

"Hmm," one villager remarked when she saw Miss Rogers with her full bag, "Thank God, me have money fuh buy what me need."

Miss Rogers ignored her.

The shop became the new meeting place for the villagers. My friends no longer came over to play while their parents chatted with Granny Shiela when they came to "borrow" a grocery item.

Many children cringed with embarrassment when they entered the shop. Mr. Hardat was slightly deaf and spoke loudly with a sibilant hiss at the end of words ending with the letter 's' and people's business was broadcast for everyone to hear.

"What yuh mother want? Flour, washing s-s-soap?" Mr. Hardat would ask loudly. It was in the shop, too, that villagers learned what was the meal for the day in a neighbour's house since "Miss Monroe" had "trusted" potatoes, curry and chicken.

All was going well until Miss Tommy fell out of favour with Mr. Hardat. I heard Miss Daisie telling Granny Shiela that Miss Tommy owed sixty-five dollars to Mr. Hardat because she usually got a "feeling" to eat some potato roti or bakes with saltfish. Since she was a good cook, her friends would stop by to "taste her hand". She enjoyed the status of being the most popular woman in the village.

Although Miss Tommy had not paid Mr. Hardat for two months, she still sent Pascal, her son, to pick up some saltfish, rice and flour from Mr. Hardat's shop. Miss Daisie was right there and reported everything to Granny Shiela who was her best friend. She dropped in for a chat at least once a day because there was so much to talk about in our village. Although Granny Shiela pretended Miss Daisie's visit was a nuisance, she fretted if she didn't see her for a day or two. Obviously, this would only happen when they had a falling out.

The narrative went like this: "Plenty people ben in de shop and everybody talking at de same time...."

"Trust me ah pound of sugar, Mr. Hardat."

"Quarter pint cooking oil Mr. Hardat."

"Two cakes of washing soap and a bag of soap powder, Mr. Hardat."

Pascal wormed past the crowd of women and two old men who were demanding a "flatie" of rum and two bottles of coke. He spoke as loudly as he could.

"Good afternoon, Mr. Hardat. Mammie say she wan three pounds rice, two pounds saltfish and four pounds flour, please and thanks Mr. Hardat."

Mr. Hardat peered at Pascal. With his grey hair and grey beard, and his rounded black spectacles perched on his pointed nose, he looked like a chubby panda.

"And what is your mother's name?" Mr. Hardat asked kindly.

"Miss Tommy," Pascal replied.

Mr. Hardat's kind and avuncular demeanour changed instantly. "Tell your mother," Mr. Hardat said loudly, "she owes-s-s me sixty-five dollars-s-s-s. No credit today, she must pay right away."

A stifled burst of laughter came from one of the women and the others began snickering behind their hands.

"Is how she like play rich," Miss Mildred said. She was peeved because Mrs. Tommy no longer came over to borrow a tin of milk or a cup of flour. She was also unable to gossip about what she saw in Mrs. Tommy's house whenever she went over to "taste" something Miss Tommy had cooked.

Pascal slinked out of the shop, shoulders hunched and his eyes fixed on the ground as the group of persons burst into uproarious laughter at what Miss Mildred had said. Miss Tommy was too embarrassed to send back for credit until she had cleared the bill, and she shamefacedly began chatting with her neighbours asking once again to borrow a pound of rice. I enjoyed the way Miss Daisie related her stories, it made me feel as though I was actually there when the incident occurred.

Guided Questions

1. What does the writer mean in this phrase, "change is inevitable"?

2. Explain clearly what makes Mrs. Sobers stand out in the village.

3. Why is the word "clarion gossiper" a suitable word to describe Miss Daisie?

4. What is the main event in this chapter and where does it take place?

5. What does the word "cringed" mean? Why do you think the young children "cringed" when they were sent to Mr. Hardat's shop?

6. "Pascal wormed his way through the crowd of women." What figure of speech is used in this statement?

7. Find the meaning of avuncular in the dictionary and then in your own words explain what an "avuncular demeanour" means.

8. Miss Mildred was "peeved". What does this word mean? Why was Miss Mildred peeved?

9. What theme is being explored in this chapter?

10. How did Mr. Hardat ensure the people owing him money paid their bills?

11. Give another word to replace these words used in the chapter: (i) peeved (ii) slinked

Discussion

Which is better, the method used by Mr. Hardat to document his sales, or the present method supermarkets use?

Has this chapter has been named appropriately.

The writer mentions that Mrs. Hardat wore a red dot in the middle of her forehead to show that she was married. This is part of Indian culture. What do people in the Caribbean do to show their marital status? Which would you prefer? Why?

What does it mean to be "honourably discharged" from the army?

Chapter Three

The Arrivals Continue!

One day I heard Granny Shiela mutter rather crossly, "Dis village will soon burst at its seams." I didn't ask her what she meant because I was sure she would tell me I was too inquisitive. It was as if Granny Shiela could see the future, because six months after Mr. Hardat arrived, Mr. Hoo Ching opened his restaurant at the corner of Lima Street. It was called Hunan Garden even though there was no garden surrounding it. Granny Shiela said the name wasn't a bad one because Hoo Ching (people hardly ever attached the respected Mr. in front of the names of villagers) had small pots of herbs on the window sills around his restaurant.

Hoo Ching was short in stature with almond eyes and a yellow tinge to his skin. He was the son of an immigrant who came to Guyana to work on the rice field. Since Hoo Ching was born in Guyana, he had assimilated to the West Indian way of life. One afternoon during a conversation between Auntie Gillie and Granny Shiela, my itching ears pricked up when Auntie Gillie said Hoo Ching had an "outside woman".

"What outside woman mean?" I pestered Granny Shiela.

"Girl, go outside and play!" she responded angrily.

Hoo Ching's wife, a Chinese national, had travelled from China specifically to marry him. She did not talk much and seemed afraid of her own shadow. No one knew where the "outside woman" came from, but both she and Mrs. Hoo Ching lived in the same apartment at the back of the restaurant. A middle-aged Indian woman ran the restaurant, collecting orders and serving customers. The daughter she had by Hoo Ching played with the children he had with his wife. This was a strange practice, as every now and then different women in the village who had children by the same man engaged in fierce quarrels or even fights.

"Ah wonder if dey does have quarrels in de house?" Miss Daisie spoke aloud, but she buttoned up her lips after one glare from Granny Shiela.

Hoo Ching did not open his restaurant early in the day; rather, business was brisk from three o'clock in the afternoon to 12 o'clock each night, including Sundays. His mixed Chinese fried rice drew the crowd because the ingredients were unique. I especially liked his chow mein. He claimed his deceased father brought the recipe from China and left it with him. The pieces of wine-red chicken, pineapple chunks and the mixture of different herbal spices ensured customers returned again and again. His sing-song Asian dialect voice was pleasing, especially to us young children.

The owner of a small local restaurant nearby was not very happy with Hoo Ching's success, Curiously though, a vicious rumour began circulating in the village: "The secret ingredient in Hoo Ching's fried rice was dog meat!" This horrified not only me, but the villagers as well. I made sure to check on our little poodle every evening to make sure he hadn't made it to Hoo Ching's pot. Our family usually bought fast food from Hoo Ching in the evenings when Auntie Gillie felt too tired to cook, but mostly on Fridays. Alicia and I looked forward to "Fast Food Fridays". After Auntie Gillie heard the rumour she expressed shock, and shuddered when she thought we might have eaten the dog meat, too! Hoo Ching's business began to fall off and the brave-hearted ones declared, "Dog meat, horse meat, cow meat...is food we eating."

This scary situation was reported to Miss Maxwell. She was a tall, strapping woman with a deep voice. People respected her, not only for her size, but she was also known to give an unbiased response to anything she heard. Her great, great grandmother was one of the founding members of Golden Grove. She felt as though the village belonged to her family, and given the increasing number of new persons coming into the village, she didn't want anyone taking advantage of the people who lived there.

Miss Daisie made her usual report. She was not only a gossip but also a storyteller. I enjoyed her storytelling!

Miss Daisie was chatting with her godson's mother in the vicinity of the restaurant one Friday morning when the harsh, grating voice of the village matriarch could be heard from far away as she strode purposefully towards Hoo Ching's shop followed by the regular thrill seekers.

"Hoo Ching, come out here," ordered Miss Maxwell.

Hoo Ching emerged from the restaurant in his customary white vest and apron, drying his hands with a kitchen towel.

"Good evening, Madam," he said, giving a little bow. "How can I help?"

"I hear say, you cooking dog meat and putting it in de fried rice," Miss Maxwell said fiercely, hands on her hips as though ready to fight.

"No Madam. No cooking doggie." Hoo Ching looked both horrified and ready to burst into tears. "I cooking chicken fly lice and mix chow mein." Hoo Ching's language deteriorated whenever he was upset or angry.

"What yuh saying?" Miss Maxwell interrupted, "Flies and lice go into yuh pot?" She was a bit hard of hearing. The crowd tittered. Miss Maxwell looked sick as she thought of the many nights she had ordered fried rice for dinner. She also looked angry enough to scuffle up Hoo Ching. Luckily, the "outside" woman came out from behind the cowering wife and children of Hoo Ching.

"Is what de problem?" she asked.

"People saying Hoo Ching does cook dog," Miss Maxwell said bristling with further outrage.

"Not true," the other woman said emphatically. "We does eat from de same pot, and I certainly won't give my chile dog to eat. Who say so?"

When Miss Maxwell turned around to find the news carrier, the crowd had diminished significantly. Those who remained looked wide-eyed at Miss Maxwell and shook their heads denying association with what was being said.

Hoo Ching became more agitated and burst into a string of unintelligible Chinese

"An hear dis. Everybody start backing away." Miss Daisie shook her head. "Den people began leaving one by one until dere was only Mrs. Maxwell left standing," she finished the report.

There was silence for a while before Miss Daisie continued.

"To tell yuh de trut, Mrs. Maxwell looked ashamed for a minute before she said gruffly, 'I sorry bout dis, eh.' She turned and walked away, attempting a dignified retreat".

Granny Shiela shook her head as though she couldn't believe what she heard. "Jealousy is a terrible ting," she muttered to herself.

"Dat reminds me of de biblical story bout de woman caught in adultery," Granny Shiela huffed out a laugh. "Remember in de New Testament, a group of men, wid big stones, brought a woman to Jesus and accused her right dere...." Granny's voice trailed off when she realised I was listening very keenly.

"Fuh true," agreed Miss Daisie.

I needed to know how that story ended so I promised myself to ask Mrs. London, my Sunday School teacher about that!

Business went back to usual at Hoo Ching restaurant and our family enjoyed Fast Food Fridays once again.

Guided Questions

1. In what way had Hoo Ching "acculturated to the West Indian way of life"?

2. What language do the Chinese people speak? Why do you think their pronunciation is different from yours?

3. Granny Shiela says the "village bursting at the seams". What figure of speech is used here. Explain in your own words what the statement means.

4. Miss Daisie "buttoned up her lips". What name is given to such statements? What does it mean?

5. Why did the young children find it pleasing when Hoo Ching spoke?

6. Describe Hoo Ching's appearance. Give one word to describe his character.

7. What does the phrase "village matriarch" mean?

8. What does Mrs. Maxwell's behaviour and language reveal about her character?

9. What does the word "flustered" mean?

Discussion

The story mentions an "outside woman". What does this mean? Do you think a woman should aspire to be the outside woman in a relationship? Explain your opinion. Is this the right way to live?

"A vicious rumour was started about Hoo Ching's restaurant". Who do you think started this rumour? Why?

The writer makes a comparison to a biblical story based on Miss Maxwell's accusation. What biblical story is this? How is this applicable?

Find out the figure of speech that usually refers to comparisons between two ideas as used in the biblical story or other stories.

What special ingredients does your mother put in her food to make it tastier?

Name other Caribbean accents that you find attractive or you dislike. Explain why you feel this way.

There are different ethnic groups mentioned in this chapter. Link their arrivals to your History lesson. What were these ethnic groups called? Why did they come to the Caribbean?

Additional Work

Research why Chinese nationals in this chapter had a problem pronouncing their "r"s. Discuss whether this situation has improved currently.

Suppose you were Hoo Ching and felt very angry with Mrs. Maxwell. Write down the Mandarin/Chinese translation to express your anger.

Role Play. Make up a short skit where you pretend to be from one of the countries mentioned so far in the book. Introduce yourselves to the rest of the class and say something about your culture.

Chapter Four

A Cultural Blend

I was playing outside in the yard when I observed a strange face. I hastily ran inside to alert Granny Shiela. "Granny Shiela," I said breathlessly. "I see a new person in the village, and he look just like Hoo Ching."

"I wonder who dat could be now?" Granny Shiela said. She came into the porch and we both watched him as he walked out of sight. I thought, *Another new face. New name to learn.*

The man's name was Chung Fat. He opened a laundromat. A Chinese national, he found it easy to relate to Hoo Ching, and they soon became best friends. Chung Fat's laundromat did not have much room, but just enough for the two big washing machines and a large dryer. I was fascinated by this. I was more accustomed to seeing Auntie Gillie, with her back bent over the tub as she scrubbed the clothes before hanging them in the sun to dry. I especially loved it when she picked up the clothes while they were warm and placed them in my arms. I would bury my face in the clothes and enjoy the crisp, clean smell.

The clients using the laundromat facilities were mostly the well-to-do from the other villages nearby. Every Saturday, the cars queued up outside the laundromat. The clients came with soiled clothing rolled up in a bundle and left with clothes in spotless condition, either in transparent plastic bags or hanging wardrobes. Sitting in the pews of our Anglican church, I would try to guess whose well-pressed clothes were compliments of Mr. Chung Fat laundromat.

At first, Auntie Gillie had reservations going to a laundromat because, like the other women in Golden Grove, she felt her hands could wash clothes far better than any machine; but once the rains came and the clothes took a long time to dry, Auntie Gillie caved in and took Uncle Tom and her clothes to Chung Fat. On Saturdays, Granny Shiela stood over Alicia instructing her how to wash clothes properly. I was excused because I was younger, so Alicia had to wash my clothes, too. I guess that was one more thing she held against me.

Rosie Perriera, a young woman in her early thirties, was next to appear in my village. She was always well-dressed and her face looked smooth and pretty. Soon, Rosie employed an American manicurist named Melinda, and Basalia, a masseuse who said she had been trained in France. No one knew how these two women arrived in Golden Grove, but they shared an apartment on the newly-built road on the eastern side of town. Quite a number of young women patronized Rosie's salon every weekend or whenever there was a holiday. I really admired the slick hairstyles. Sometimes Granny Shiela would "iron" out Alicia's hair on Sundays. Me? I was too young for that according to Granny Shiela. My hair was thick, unlike Alicia's which was nappy, and I would spitefully draw it to her attention. Alicia got her revenge when Auntie Gillie washed my hair and tried to comb out the tangles.

I took note of Mr. Abraham when he came to my village. He was a light-skinned, tall man with teeth that gleamed like ivory whenever he laughed. He said he was born in Russia.

Granny Shiela asked, "Russia not on de odder side a de world? How he reach here in Guyana?" No one knew the answer to that question.

Mr. Abraham's pawn shop, Cash for Gold Creative Jewellery, involved taking the gold jewellery of the villagers when he lent them money. When they repaid him the money, with added interest, he would return the jewellery. His shop was crammed like a beehive, noticeably on Mondays and Fridays. On Mondays the women pawned their gold chains and wedding bands to ensure they had money to buy groceries for the week; however, the men pawned their gold links late Friday evenings to accommodate their weekend gambling spree.

"I doan understand how dese people can live so hand-to-mout," Granny Shiela said crossly, as we went to visit one of her friends who was feeling under the weather. I wondered what this phrase meant as I skipped along to accommodate her longer steps. Then I observed Miss Daisie entering the pawn shop.

"Look, Miss Daisie dere, Granny," I said.

Granny Shiela sucked her teeth long and hard. "The likkle jewellery she have gwine soon disappear. She gwine spend de money and forget dat she have only tree monts to pay or Mr. Abraham gwine seize she jewels an dem."

Auntie Gillie had gifted me with a pair of gold bangles and a pair of earrings in the shape of a cluster of grapes and I fervently hoped no one in my family would pawn my gifts.

Mr. Rivers, a Portuguese man sporting two pointed gold teeth, a ponytail, three heavy gold chains around his neck, and two broad gold bracelets adorning his left wrist, drove into our village one Sunday morning. He took up residence in a large house two streets away from where we lived. A fleet of six cars lined the street next to his house while the one he drove was parked in his garage. No one knew where he got the money to buy these cars, but he settled quite comfortably in the village. Five men, who claimed they came from Providence Village, worked with him as chauffeurs. These cars provided services such as emergency trips to the hospital and driving around the men who came from the gold fields.

Every young child in my village knew that our country possessed gold. After all, some of the men who lived in our village worked in the gold fields in the Cuyuni and Mazaruni District. Found in the vicinity of Bartica, on the west bank of the Essequibo river in Guyana, the villages in this small town got their names from the two rivers, Cuyuni and Mazaruni, near to them.

The men who worked in the gold fields were referred to locally as "pork-knockers." When these pork-knockers came to our village after some months in the gold field, they behaved like visiting dignitaries. They paid for personal chauffeurs, and the windows of the cars were wound down so everyone could admire them. They waved to us as if they were some kind of royalty acknowledging an admiring audience. For days after their visits, I would pester Auntie Gillie asking whether I could be a pork-knocker when I grew up. I would practice waving to people as I drove my "car" at the back of the house.

Mr. Greaves arrived in our village with the intention of establishing a funeral parlour. All we knew was that he came from a small European country (no one knew its name) and specialized in "posh" funerals. People had such fear and respect for the dead that men took of their hats whenever the passed the parlour. There was hushed silence inside when a funeral service took place.

He also constructed the most modern graves. Rather than grave diggers toiling in the hot sun to dig the required six feet in which coffins would be lowered, Mr. Greaves asked the grave diggers to dig out three feet in the soil. Then they enclosed the hole with a concrete structure that lasted much longer than the mounds of earth that were difficult to locate after some years had passed. Interestingly, the funeral parlour was just next to the Anglican church with its massive cemetery.

Not surprisingly, Mr. Greaves did not have many friends, as people were quite reluctant to visit him since he lived above the funeral parlour. Not only were the empty coffins on display in his showroom, but also the bodies of the dearly departed who would be buried the following day. Granny Shiela and Auntie Gillie, towing me along, walked on the opposite side of the road whenever we passed that way. On one occasion Uncle Tom came home spluttering with anger and fright. He had been walking gingerly past the funeral parlour when Mr. Greaves engaged him in a conversation for half an hour in front of the parlour. Granny Shiela told Uncle Tom to have a bath instantly with some salt and lime juice. She warned him against answering anyone who called his name that night. It was the first time I saw Uncle Tom go to bed so early.

Guided Questions

1. Explain why the title of this chapter is appropriate.

2. The writer mentions a number of services that were now being offered in Golden Grove. Name these services.

3. Identify two major themes referred to in this chapter and give the relevant examples.

4. In your own words explain what "collateral" means. Was this good business practice? Why? Why not?

5. There are five main senses that are used to create imagery. What are these senses? Find a phrase that appeals to at least four of these senses.

6. What does the idiom "hand-to-mouth" mean?

Discussion

Why is the Caribbean usually referred to as a "melting pot"?

Research what job a masseuse does. Do you think it is a good career choice?

Does a pawn shop exist in your country? What do people do when they need quick cash? Is this good business practice?

How do you think Mr. Rivers earned money when the pork-knockers were not in the village?

Research which businesses use a system of "credit or trust".

Chapter Five

Innocence Lost!

I learnt early that I could not believe everything I heard; that life was not the golden bubble I thought it was. The incident I want to share occurred just as I turned four years old and left me feeling rather disillusioned. The valuable lesson I learned was that things are not always what they seem.

Christmas was the most joyous occasion for me. I knew from the songs we listened to that Santa Claus usually visited at this time of the year with lots of presents for all the children. The preschool I attended taught us all about it. And Aunty Gillie always reminded me, "If you don't behave, Santa Claus would not bring you any Christmas presents."

"Where does Santa Claus live?" I had asked wide-eyed. "Why is only coming at Christmas?" I was always asking who, why, where, when, and how.

Auntie Gillie brought out a large book and pointed to a fat, red-cheeked man with white flowing beard, dressed in bright red clothes. His smile was wide, and his face was as bright as a full moon. He was holding some funny horses that had horns. He seemed as though he never had any worries at all.

"Santa lives in a country filled with snow and he travels in the sky on these reindeer." Auntie Gillie responded, pointing to the funny horses.

I listened attentively as Auntie Gillie explained that snow looked just like the shaved ice the snow cone man sold from his cart, cocking my head to the side just like my kindergarten teacher did from time to time. Every time Auntie Gillie bought a snow cone for me, I pretended I was eating snow, but with a rainbow of colour as the condensed milk and the red, blue and green colours merged.

That year Uncle Tom received a large bonus from his workplace and promised to buy Christmas presents for the whole family. Auntie Gillie took me to town and showed me a wide array of toys. She asked me which one I wanted so she could tell Santa Claus I had been very good. My excitement to see what Santa would bring me grew and grew until I "wet" my bed for two consecutive nights three weeks before Christmas.

Auntie Gillie was not amused. "Like you getting backwards or what?" she asked angrily as she changed the bed sheets. "You stopped wetting your bed when you were two years old."

"Sorry Auntie Gillie," I responded. "I am 'toxicated with impatience." I had been waiting for the longest while to use that word. It made me feel so important.

"Wha...what?" Auntie Gillie spluttered. "Where you heard those words?" Auntie Gillie could not understand how as four-year-old child I had such an extensive vocabulary. Little did she know that Uncle Tom would regularly have me repeating some "big words". Then he would try to explain what they meant.

"Uncle Tom said that Mr. Mason gets 'toxicated every Friday night, and sometimes during the week he is impatient for Friday to come," I explained carefully.

"That's what comes when small children grow up with only adults in a house," Auntie Gillie grumbled to herself. "Y'all start talking like adults too."

My excitement about Christmas did not lessen. I just knew that most of the presents would be for me since Alicia was always getting into trouble. She couldn't blame me for telling on her when she left drinking glasses in our room and threw pieces of food under the bed. She surely didn't expect me to sweep the room. I wasn't the one that kept it dirty!

I was the first one who woke up on Christmas morning. I scampered down to the huge Christmas tree in the living room. And there I found seven gaily wrapped presents. I heard Granny Shiela pottering around in the kitchen.

"Granny! Granny!" I squealed, "Look what Santa bought for me!" I jumped up and down with excitement as I pointed to the gifts.

Granny Shiela gave me a bear hug. "Merry Christmas! Let's see wha Santa brought for yuh," she said and gave me three of the presents. I tore off the wrappers and inspected a large doll, a floor puzzle with five hundred pieces and three books. Then I looked expectantly at the other five or more gifts remaining under the Christmas tree.

"We're not opening them now?" I asked in bewilderment.

"dey are for de rest of de family," Granny Shiela explained. "Now run along and show de others wha Santa got yuh."

The rest of the family, I thought. *I'm sure Auntie Gillie said Santa only brought gifts for good boys and girls. And I have been very good! And where is my present from Uncle Tom and Auntie Gillie?*

I crept into the study, opened the big book and sat looking at Santa Claus picture for a long time. When Granny Shiela could not find me, she tracked me down to the study where she found me crying my heart out as I looked at the pictures in the book.

"Why yuh cryin'?" Granny Shiela asked. She was puzzled. "Doan yuh like yer presents?"

But I cried even louder. Granny Shiela put me to sit down, dried my eyes and said sternly, "Now yuh stop dat crying, young lady. Wha is de matter wid yuh?" By this time the rest of the family had crowded into the study.

"Only Santa Claus loves me," I began blubbering again, "Nobody else loves me. See, is he alone bring presents for me. No one else."

Granny Shiela was dumbfounded, Uncle Tom shook his head, Alicia bowed her head hiding a smirk and Auntie Gillie was lost for words.

"You fix dis Gillie," Granny said bustling out of the room as she muttered, "Dis girl growin' up too fast."

Uncle Tom and Alicia left so it was just Auntie Gillie and me. Auntie Gillie gave a huge sigh before she said, "Let me explain something to you, Sue."

There she revealed that Santa Claus did not really exist, but it was a made-up story that was told to young children to help them behave well.

"But if Santa did not bring the gifts, who brought them?" I was confused.

"Uncle Tom and I bought them," Auntie Gillie looked a little ashamed. "We couldn't give you all the gifts. Everyone deserves a gift at Christmas." She was trying really hard to make me understand.

I felt betrayed and heartbroken to think the stories told by Auntie Gillie were untrue. And my teachers too didn't tell the truth! I wondered if my friends knew.

Later that evening when we were in our room Alicia accused me of being so selfish that I had wanted all the gifts.

"You think the world revolves around you?" she asked.

I could not answer; but it was the first time I realised that adults told lies. I was confused too! How could Auntie Gillie keep telling me to speak the truth, when she didn't do so herself? It was in my teenage years I realised that the older generation wanted us to find ways to express our love for each other and see the goodness in the world. Most importantly, it was their way to get us to use our imagination.

Guided Questions

1. What is the major theme in this story?
2. What does the word "disillusioned" mean?
3. Briefly explain what was the disillusionment the narrator encountered.
4. What excuse does she give for adults not telling the truth?
5. Identify at least one piece of imagery and one figure of speech used in this story.

Discussion

Are children today smarter than children long ago?

Do you think parents "deceive" their children deliberately when they are young? What word would be appropriate to describe what parents do?

Additional Work

Revisit your word bank. Have you added new vocabulary?

Chapter Six

Moving Forward

As the village grew, the government added a small primary school and a health centre to accommodate the increasing population. Golden Grove was soon separated into three distinct areas—the seediest side, the swankiest side, and the steamiest side. The villagers ended up in the part of the village where they felt most comfortable. I would have preferred to live in the swankiest side of the village, but I didn't have a choice!

The seediest side consisted of houses built parallel to a slab of concrete wall that separated the Atlantic Ocean from the village. Everyone called it the "seawall". Built to prevent the surges of the Atlantic Ocean from flooding the village, the concrete wall was both horizontal and vertical. To access the top of the wall, we had to cross over on a broad plank in order to take an afternoon stroll and enjoy the sea breeze. The seawall was where everyone congregated on holidays. A deep trench covered by a plank gave us access to the seawall. The trench was always full of water that spilled over from the Atlantic Ocean whenever it was high tide. We were never allowed to cross the plank alone for fear we would fall over and drown.

The houses were roughly constructed as most of the men in this area were either masons or carpenters. Since they were neither schooled in the art of carpentry or masonry, the men paid no attention to design or luxury; they simply wanted a roof to cover their heads and protect them from the weather. Other men travelled to a quarry two villages away to break up stones—back-breaking work with little pay, but it was better than nothing. Most women were housewives.

Since money was hard to come by, the villagers in the seediest side found other means of dealing with the difficult life they had. Many evenings there were domino matches among the men; those who were not playing placed bets on the winner. Heated quarrels broke out frequently; flashing police lights appeared and blaring sirens were often heard in the area. I heard Granny Shiela and Miss Daisie talking about the people who lived there.

"You doan see is mainly de people who are "poverty stricken", drunkards and dem who not right in dey head living in dat side a de village," Granny Shiela said, wrinkling her nose in disgust.

"If people offer me ah million dallars, I not going dere to live," Miss Daisie replied. "I cyant understand why poor people cyant behave demself."

Unfortunately, Alicia and I had to walk through a part of the seediest side of the village to get to school. Auntie Gillie warned us repeatedly to come home from school immediately after its dismissal. According to Granny Shiela, "Stones nah have eyes! So if alyuh know what good fuh yuh, walk fast as possible when yuh have to pass tru dere."

Rich people lived on swankiest side of the village. Their manor houses mirrored those in England with large windows and beautiful gardens and all similar in design with circular driveways. Their porches sported large potted palms, and bright red poinsettia flowers.

These houses once belonged to families who owned sugar plantations in Guyana but had moved back to England to live. The new owners were bank managers, businessmen, and retirees. Their chihuahuas lived indoors, and the wives of these men—dressed in lily-white short and halter tops, or flowing kaftans—walked them out regularly. Most of the houses in this area were enclosed in a compound with fences painted white. A security guard gave permission to persons who wanted to visit the compound and monitored them very closely.

When I was in Kindergarten my best friend was Thandi. Her parents came from Holland, and they lived in the compound on the swankiest side of the village. Her father drove to work in the capital, so he would drop Thandi to school early in the morning. Her mother, who was a stay-at-home-mom, was responsible for getting her back home. Since we lived a stone's throw away from the swankiest side, Thandi's mother saw nothing wrong with her daughter walking home from school with us. On one occasion I was allowed to enter the compound with my friend, while Alicia waited outside the gate.

The residents, mostly the women, were sitting on their porches. One woman smiled at me, called me over and gave me a candy. When I left the compound I showed it to Alicia before I put it in my bag. I planned on enjoying the tart taste later on in the evening. I should have known it would not work out that way.

As soon as we got home Alicia began, "Granny Shiela, Sue was begging people for candies. If you search her bag, you will find it."

"She's lying Granny," I began but I didn't finish my protest, as Granny Shiela grabbed my bag and found the candy I had tucked away between my books. Then the scolding began.

"Alyuh children does make yuh family feel shame. Why alyuh you have to behave as if yuh so hungry?"

"Is not me, Granny. Is Sue," Alicia was quick to say. I didn't say a word. Alicia was upset because she had asked me for a piece of the rock candy, and I refused to share.

"What were you girls doing in that area?" Auntie Gillie asked.

"One of my friends live there," I responded.

"Hmph. Doan let me hear anytin' like dis again," Granny Shiela warned.

My voice was almost non-existent as I gave a negative response. I never went back into the compound. I would say goodbye to Thandi as soon as we got to her gate.

The third section of our village was called the "steamiest side". In this area stores sold revealing clothes such as mini dresses and transparent night clothes and clinging leather pants. A few discotheques played soft music on week days and loud music on the weekends. The bars, unlike the seediest side of the village, were not called rum shops. They sold imported wine and other alcoholic beverages, and a security guard was employed to ensure there was no unseemly behaviour. On weekends, well-dressed and elegant people attended the parties held there. We heard the music loud and clear in the distance and sometimes, I could see Uncle Tom tapping his feet as though he wanted to break into dance moves. At times, he put a record on the gramophone. When the slow tunes began, he pulled Auntie Gillie out of the armchair and waltzed her across the room. I was not left out because Uncle Tom would let me stand on his feet and I, too, became a part of their enchanted circle. Alicia in most cases was in her room "studying".

We did not live in the seediest side of the village; neither did we live on the swankiest side of the village. Our house was located on the outskirts of the seediest side just three streets away from the swankiest side. Granny Shiela called the house in which we lived a "cut above de rest". There were three bedrooms upstairs, a dining room, and a kitchen. Alicia and I shared a bedroom; so did Auntie Gillie and Uncle Tom. Granny Shiela had a room all by herself. Most importantly, our house was one of the few houses with an inside toilet, and a porch that gave Granny Shiela a chance to observe and comment on who was walking past and what was happening in the village.

Alicia and I attended the Golden Grove Primary School and had to be well-groomed, as Granny Shiela kept mumbling, "Yuh need to show yuh have class." She pointed to the children who went to school barefooted and told us we ought to be glad we had shoes to wear. According to Granny Shiela, "When yuh walk barefoot all de time, you foot will get broad like planks."

The teachers at the school were old and strict. They taught us Bible stories twice every day, and we learned our tables through drills. The strap was frequently applied to the backs of the children who did not listen or memorize their tables. I hated to be embarrassed and had a low tolerance for "licks" so I applied myself to my work. My teacher, Miss Squires, loved me. The other children called me the teacher's pet, but I was the only one who asked questions.

When Auntie Gillie attended school meetings, the teachers would say, "Sue is such a joy to teach. We like her inquiring mind. She will go far in life."

Alicia, who was in Standard six, was dubbed rude and uncooperative. She had no best friend because she was not a friendly person. I could understand why this was so, since she hardly wanted to speak with me even though we shared the same room.

Guided Questions

1. The village was divided into three separate areas. Name these areas.

2. What scandalized Miss Daisie about the men in one of these areas? Why do you think she was scandalized?

3. Explain the phrase "tight-lipped".

4. Give an example of a simile and onomatopoeia used in this chapter.

5. What does a "cut above the rest" mean?

6. Which area did the narrator like best? Why?

7. Identify a theme used in this chapter.

8. In your own words, say what makes each area unique.

Discussion

Examine the seediest side of the village. Is there an area in your country that can be termed as "seedy"?

How can an area improve its mode of operations so that it is no longer associated with negative behaviour?

Do you think that the teachers should have used the strap to get children to learn? What was your experience in primary school? What else could the teachers have done to get the children to learn their tables?

Chapter Seven

My First Adventure!

Whenever Miss Daisie visited Georgetown, the capital city, she told us about everything she had seen and heard. To Alicia and me, it sounded like it was a foreign country as Auntie Gillie had never taken us there.

One day Miss Daisie stopped by to show Granny Shiela what she bought when she went to Georgetown.

She sat down in the porch. "Lemme ketch me breat'," Miss Daisie said, continuing as though she wasn't tired at all. "Shiela, if yuh see some massive pumpkin! I swear to God say dddddddey look like dem big boulder dat does roll down from de quarry in Verity. And dem market people too tief. Dey selling one slice ah pumpkin for a whole shilling!" Granny Shiela looked scandalized.

"Where is Georgetown?" I asked.

Miss Daisie looked at me in surprise. "Yuh Auntie never tek yuh dere?"

I shook my head just as Auntie Gillie came up the steps. Miss Daisie continued the conversation as though Auntie Gillie had been there all the time.

"Gillie, why yuh never take dem children to Georgetown? Yuh want dem grow up dotish and backward?"

Auntie Gillie looked irritated. "Miss Daisie Georgetown is a big place and..."

Miss Daisie interrupted, "Just hold dey hand tight. Alicia is not a baby, and Sue is now what six, seven years. You gwine wait till dey get old and grey to go into de capital city of Guyana?"

"We will see," Auntie Gillie muttered before she escaped into the house.

After that conversation, I asked Auntie Gillie religiously when she would take us to Georgetown, until she got so fed up and responded, "Easter time!"

I jumped up and down with glee. "Uncle Tom. We are going to Georgetown."

"We are?" Uncle Tom asked.

"Yes. Auntie Gillie said we will go at Easter time."

Uncle Tom looked at me, doubtfully. "I will have to discuss it with your aunt," he replied.

The next morning I asked Granny Shiela, "Granny, how long before Easter?"

"Is two weeks away," Granny Shiela said.

Uncle Tom sighed. "Sue won't stop asking till Gillie to take them. Georgetown is a big place. She better hold their hands tightly."

"That's what Miss Daisie said," I piped up. Alicia rolled her eyes, and I stuck out my tongue at her.

Auntie Gillie finally consented to taking us into Georgetown—the big city—on Easter Saturday. Uncle Tom said he couldn't accompany us because he was called in at the last minute to work the day shift at the Brewery. "I can't wait to retire," he muttered crossly.

Auntie Gillie packed a snack box since she planned for us to go to the Botanical Gardens for a mini picnic. She also intended to get one of the early buses for our trip into town because of the distance.

"Hold Sue hand tight," Granny Shiela warned, "You know she don't keep quiet."

"Mother I am not a child," Auntie Gillie snapped in response. "You should be telling the two of them to stick close to me."

When the time came for us to go, Granny Shiela said, "Take dem by de museum and by Fogarty Store. Dey got some nice children clothes and books, and yuh can walk out de back door of Fogarty straight to de museum."

"What the museum got Granny?" I asked.

"Wait and you go see," was her puzzling response.

In the bus, we were squeezed like sardines. Its swaying movement made me almost want to throw up, but one look at Auntie Gillie's face made me swallow down the rising bile in my throat. I would not have put it past her to take me back home immediately.

Georgetown is massive—no other word will do! I felt like an insect surrounded by gigantic trees. The buildings went high into the air and people hurried past us, their eyes staring straight ahead and their faces rather serious. The crowd was so thick at times, I could hardly breathe. I held tightly to Auntie Gillie's skirt and Alicia's hand, but both of them showed irritation—Auntie Gillie was irritated because I was creasing up her skirt, while Alicia didn't want to be touched.

"You want to pull off my skirt," Auntie Gillie's voice was accusatory. Alicia wriggled her fingers out of my clasp, muttering, "You squeezing my hand too tight."

When we got to Fogarty's building, my eyes opened wide with wonder. "How will we get up there?" I asked Auntie Gillie. Fogarty's was the namesake for a department store in Guyana opened by a well-known English businessman. Everyone shopped there.

"There is an elevator," Auntie Gillie replied, "but I don't trust those things. We will take the steps."

There were seven floors in all, but by the time we got to our destination on the fourth floor, Auntie Gillie was gasping for breath. Luckily, there were dining sets and living room suites on display. Knowing that salespeople don't like customers sitting on their new chairs, Auntie Gillie looked around quickly before she plopped into the plush, comfortable depths of a chair.

"We will walk around just now," Auntie Gillie panted. "Let me catch my breath."

Alicia sat down in chair while I climbed up into another. The chair was soft and comfortable. I felt so tired because of the excitement of travelling and walking up those steps, that I fell asleep. When I awoke, I saw neither Auntie Gillie nor Alicia. My eyes filled with tears, but I forced them back.

I got down from the chair and wandered around. There were so many half-dressed men and women standing around, I became curious. I walked boldly up to one of them. "Why aren't you dressed properly?" I asked politely, but the woman didn't answer. Next, I turned to the man and looking up at him I asked, "Did you see my Auntie?"

The next thing I felt was a hard pinch on my arms. "Sue, why are you speaking to a mannequin?" Alicia hissed. I began wailing loudly and the shoppers turned to look at us. Auntie Gillie came bustling up.

"What is the matter with you?" she whispered fiercely. "You want to embarrass me? Alicia I told you to keep an eye on your cousin. I just leave you for a while and now...

"She was speaking to the mannequin," Alicia interrupted, "I was trying to get her to sit back down where you left her."

"But Auntie Gillie," I protested, "There was no one here when I woke up. I was looking for you."

Auntie Gillie turned to Alicia with a fierce scowl. "Alicia," she said sternly, "did you leave Sue sleeping there alone?"

Alicia didn't answer.

Auntie Gillie muttered crossly, "Let's go down on the second floor." Down the stairs we went into a world of fantasy. There were toys for children arranged beautifully on the floor. "Stay close to me," Auntie Gillie warned, and I really intended to do so, but she was taking so long because she met a school friend and stopped to chat.

When I glanced to my right, there were thousands of books! I eased away towards the books on display. Alicia stared at me.

"You are such a pest," she hissed angrily. "Sometimes I wish you would just disappear."

"I will tell Auntie Gillie what you said," I responded. "You are really mean."

Alicia shrugged her shoulders, then walked away from me. I was glad to see her go. I darted towards the shelves crammed with different kinds of books. I saw a shelf with the words "CHILDREN BOOKS". I walked closer. No one paid me any mind, so I walked farther and farther and was soon hidden by the tall shelves. I came to a corner of the room that was secluded with book shelves just at my height, crammed with children's books. The pictures were beautiful. I put down one book and picked up another. There was a little chair next to a shelf of books, so I sat down to read one of my favourite books, *The Little Red Hen.* I did not realize I had spent so long there until I heard a woman speaking nearby.

"I don't understand some people! They don't realize children can get lost in a store of this size."

"Who is the little girl?" another voice enquired.

"Some chile named Sumitra Gallenger," the first woman responded.

I jumped up quickly knocking over the chair. "That's my name," I said loudly.

One of the women gave a shriek and held her breast.

"This must be the little girl," the other woman said, running forward to grab me.

"Oww!" I responded, "You are holding me too tight. I want my Auntie Gillie."

The woman kept her grip on me, so I began to wail in protest.

A crowd had gathered, and some people began to say, "That must be the girl."

Another woman said, "Sometimes, dey does tief people children in dis country yuh know."

A man declared, "Call security."

Soon the security arrived, accompanied by Auntie Gillie and Alicia, who looked as if she had been crying.

Without saying a word to me, Auntie Gillie rushed across and delivered a slap to the woman holding my hand. The woman reeled back in shock. She let go my hand. I ran quickly to Auntie Gillie. I was crying in earnest from confusion and fright.

Everyone began to speak at the same time, so it took a while before the matter was cleared up. Auntie Gillie looked ashamed of herself as she apologized to the "Good Samaritan".

Turning to the lady, Auntie Gillie muttered, "People were talking all kinds of things. I heard the word "kidnapped" and panicked. You can slap me back if you wish."

The woman was furious, but she didn't say a word. Her friend on the other hand said, "You see what kindness does get you Dorothy. I hope you learn yuh lesson. Next time, let people solve dey own problem." Then they hurried away.

Auntie Gillie was so shaken, she called off our visit to the museum and took the first bus she found.

"Alicia, you have some explaining to do," Auntie Gillie said.

"Yes," I piped up. "Alicia said she…"

"Be quiet!" Auntie Gillie's voice thundered.

We returned home rather subdued.

Granny Shiela was waiting for our report when we arrived. "How was…?" she began with a smile.

Without missing a beat, Auntie Gillie said, "Don't ask," before she went into the house. She stayed in her room for the rest of the evening with a rag soaked in soothing lotion draped on her forehead. Alicia told Granny Shiela to ask me all about our day, before she rushed into our room and slammed the door.

"Granny, we had such an adventure," I began. "I got lost and somebody found me. Then Auntie Gillie got into a fight."

"Wha'… wha'… what?" Granny Shiela hollered, "Gillie!" but Auntie Gillie did not respond, and Granny Shiela had to wait until Uncle Tom came home to hear all about our adventure into town.

Guided Questions

1. Where was the setting of this story?

2. Using information from the story, give three reasons why Auntie Gillie finally decided to take the narrator into the city.

3. Identify and write down two figures of speech used in this story. Explain why they are effective.

4. The narrator mentions the "Good Samaritan". Where else have you heard this phrase? How could the woman be regarded as the "Good Samaritan"?

5. Why did Alicia pinch the narrator? Was she right to do so?

6. Why did Auntie Gillie panic?

7. To what extent was Alicia to blame for what happened?

Discussion

If you were the woman Auntie Gillie had slapped, how would you have responded?

Is Sue to be blamed for what happened at the end of the story? Give reasons for your answer.

Was the lady's friend right when she told her friend (Dorothy) to allow people to solve their own problems? Why or why not

Activity

Imagine you are Auntie Gillie, write a letter of apology to the lady whom you had slapped.

Chapter Eight

Brown Joe

I think every family should have a pet, whether it is a dog, cat, or rabbit. I asked on numerous occasions if we could get another dog. Our poodle Chooloo died after it had wandered out of our yard and eaten something. Auntie Gillie was heartbroken when she found out it was poison the neighbour had scattered in her yard to get rid of the rat infestation. She blamed herself for not being for careful, as she had not latched the gate properly.

Whenever I walked past the compound of the swankiest side of the village and saw the women strolling with their chihuahuas on a leash, I asked Auntie Gillie if she had changed her mind about getting a pet. The response was always, "Stop bothering me and go find something to do."

Fate took a hand in the situation so I could get my wish. Whenever he passed by the house, I would call out to Mr. Winston, a man who had a flock of goats. "Good morning Mr. Winston."

"You are a very respectful girl," Mr. Winston would say or, "Good morning my pretty girl."

Winston told Uncle Tom all about how much money he made from raising animals. I loved looking at the frisky kids and listening to the conversation that swirled around. Even Mr. Preddy, Granny Shiela's friend, a widower who lived not too far from us, often wandered down and joined in the conversation. One day, I saw a brown goat trotting behind Mr. Preddy as he came to visit Granny Shiela.

"Dis is a gift for me little fren who is a very smart girl," Mr. Preddy said with a smile. "Mr. Winston sent it for yuh."

I was pleased. The goat and I were almost the same height, and the little horns were not very sharp.

"It will be my pet. I'm really glad I have one now!" I exclaimed.

"Preddy, why are yuh giving Sue dis goat? You don't know ram goat does butt?" Granny Shiela was not amused. "What we want wid a goat?"

Mr. Preddy ignored her. I named my new friend Brown Joe and enjoyed him chasing behind me, until one day he butt me down. I fell into a little mud puddle and ran crying to Auntie Gillie because I had scraped my knees. After that incident, Auntie Gillie asked Uncle Tom to tie out Brown Joe every morning across the road on an abandoned property overrun with grass and weeds. I would play with my pet in the afternoons, and he didn't butt me down again. Instead, whenever Brown Joe saw me, he would run up to me, give me a gentle butt and allow me to scratch behind his ear. I really enjoyed romping with him after school.

Uncle Tom did not experience the same fondness that I had for Brown Joe.

"Why can't Alicia and Sue tie out the goat?" Uncle Tom asked. "It will teach them to be responsible."

Granny Shiela said that tying out goats was a man's job, and Alicia and I had to prepare for school. Since Uncle Tom didn't work during the day, he was given the task.

Brown Joe made it a game to butt down Uncle Tom especially at evenings.

"I don't know why we get this goat in the first place. Ram goats does smell bad, they always butt, and this goat is stunted. Since we get it and for all the grass it eating, it isn't growing. It will be worthless for breeding purposes. Every morning I have to tie out the goat, and the thing is, it doesn't even belong to me." Uncle Tom complained.

"It just playing with you, Uncle Tom," I tried to explain but to no avail.

Every day, morning and evenings, Brown Joe butted Uncle Tom. Whenever Uncle Tom appeared with grass sticking out from his head or with grass stains on his pants, he quarrelled bitterly with Granny Shiela about getting rid of the goat. "We could kill it and sell the meat," Uncle Tom advised.

I begged him not to do so, and Auntie Gillie added her protest as well. "It is Sue's pet," she said. "How can we eat a pet?"

We were at school when the incident occurred, and it was only after all the noise and drama had taken place that Granny Shiela told us about it. It went like this.

It was a Monday morning after Auntie Gillie returned from the market, Uncle Tom came into the kitchen, looked around surreptitiously and said, "Gillie, I have a confession to make."

Immediately, Auntie Gillie thought of the young woman who would call Tom for a "chat" because she was having "problems" with her plumbing or her cupboard door. Auntie Gillie said, "I hope you are not going to tell me anything about Judisha. I don't know why you can't see she has her sights on you. I will not tolerate a cheating husband."

Uncle Tom gave a forbearing sigh, "It's not about Judisha and I told you we are not having an affair. I am too old for this nonsense".

My ears perked up at the word "affair". I was going to pester Alicia until she told me what it meant.

"Well, tell me," Auntie Gillie said grudgingly.

Uncle Tom began hesitantly, "Yesterday, Winston was passing by with Mr. Veira, the butcher. When they see Brown Joe, they suggested it is best to kill him because he won't grow anymore. The butcher offered me ninety dollars and a piece of the mutton."

"You killed Brown Joe?" Auntie Gillie said disbelievingly. "What will you tell Sue?"

"I didn't kill it," Uncle Tom said defensively.

"Lord Jesus!" Auntie Gillie. "Where did you put the mutton?"

"It's in the lower part of the freezer." Uncle Tom muttered before he added, "Is not you who does get butt down every day. I'm too old for that. All you and Shiela does do when I come upstairs limping is laugh. Old people say, 'What is joke fuh school children is dead fuh crapaud.' Y'all don't realise I could get damaged badly."

"All right. All right!" Auntie Gillie said trying to console him. "But you will have to tell Sue." Granny Shiela sat quietly and listened in to their conversation.

For some reason, I didn't look for Brown Joe when I came home late from Brownies on Tuesday or Reading Club meeting on Wednesday afternoon. Thursday and Friday were hectic days with Granny Shiela's diabetes reading sky-rocketing. I did not go outside to play because I was busy wiping Granny Shiela's brows. She was sweating profusely. Auntie Gillie had to monitor her closely, so she did not fall into a coma. I was afraid my Granny Shiela would die! By Friday night, the worst had passed.

Alicia and I were allowed to go the library on Saturday morning for our usual Reading Club meetings. I read books to the children younger than me, and Alicia read to the children who were my age. Auntie Gillie was unable to go to the weekend market. She whispered to Uncle Tom, "I will have to curry the mutton for lunch this Sunday, but I am not eating Brown Joe."

Auntie Gillie had invited one of the needy children in the neighbourhood for lunch after church. She explained that God had blessed us with a little more than enough and we should be willing to share with the less fortunate. The appetizing smell of curried mutton wafted in the kitchen merging with the smell of baked macaroni pie and Spanish rice. Auntie Gillie set the table, and filled six plates with food. However, on her plate she only placed the curried potatoes—no meat.

After Uncle Tom said grace, everyone dug into their meals. Anselm, the visitor smacked his lips while I licked my spoon. Uncle Tom was eating with gusto, Granny Shiela had taken out her dentures and was sucking on a bone, while Alicia ate daintily. As Auntie Gillie looked at this surreal picture of her family eating their pet goat, a fit of giggles took hold of her, and she couldn't stop laughing.

"Why are you laughing Auntie Gillie?" I asked suspiciously. Auntie Gillie was almost hysterical by this time. Suddenly, as though a lightbulb had gone on, I asked, "Why isn't there any meat in your plate Auntie Gillie? Oh God, Brown Joe! We are eating Brown Joe!" I screamed.

Confusion reigned. Anselm burst into tears. He did not know why he was crying, but he didn't want to give up his appetizing plate of food. Alicia was quite matter of fact about the issue. As she put it, "Food is food." But I couldn't stop crying. After all, Brown Joe was my pet, and I had a right to decide if he should be killed or not. Two weeks it took before I touched any meat.

"So you is a vegetarian now?" Alicia asked with a sneer in her voice. I wished I could smother her!

I didn't reply. The third week was month end, when Uncle Tom usually came home with a bucket of fried chicken and five bags of chips.

As Auntie Gillie set the table with the food, she asked me, "Are you still off your meat?"

"Kinda," I muttered, my eyes fixed on the mouth-watering, brown, crisp, and spicy chicken.

"What you mean kinda?"Alicia demanded. "Is either you want or don't want."

"If you insist," I said, sitting down at the table and reaching for a plate, "I guess I will have to eat it."

But it took me a long time to forget my first pet and how I had eaten him! It always gives me the shivers.

Guided Questions

1. How many new characters are mentioned in this story?

2. Why was Uncle Tom given the job of tying out Brown Joe?

3. What reason does Uncle Tom give for not tying out the goat?

4. What does the phrase "eating with gusto" mean?

5. Think of the two stories you have read so far based on disillusionment. Which one do you think is the worst the narrator experienced?

6. Why do you think Alicia is being so mean to the narrator?

7. Gender roles is one of the themes mentioned in this story, find an example of it.

Discussion

Is it morally wrong to eat an animal you have reared as a pet?

How does the idea of ownership of an animal and emotional attachment to the animal influence our dietary choices?

Granny Shiela and Uncle Tom referred to two sayings that the older people made. Explain what they mean.

Discuss any other sayings you may have heard from the older generation.

Word Bank

Surreptitiously

Profusely

Forbearing

Hysterical

Grudgingly

Tolerate

Chapter Nine

Those Rumbo Chicken!

My interaction with animals continued during my primary school days particularly with the chickens Uncle Tom brought home one day. Three black hens and one rooster! Granny Shiela was glad about this. In those days, eggs were not sold from a hatchery. Instead, people reared their chickens and got their fresh eggs from the "yard fowl", which they claimed were much healthier.

"Where did you get those chickens from Uncle Tom?" I asked curiously.

"A friend gave me," he replied.

"You want to start rearing chickens now?" Auntie Gillie joined the conversation.

"Is not de odder day you say not you again wid any animal after de Browne Joe story?" Granny Shiela put in her bit, too.

"I don't have to look after them," Uncle Tom said testily. "We have enough space in the yard for them to run around, and when we throw out the left-over rice, they will eat. And besides, their eggs are healthier than the ones you buy in the supermarket. Do you know the chickens that lay those eggs are pumped up with injections to make them grow and lay eggs?"

That silenced both Granny Shiela and Auntie Gillie.

One day a second rooster appeared and joined the menagerie. Uncle Tom was quite happy. Soon our yard was filled with squawking chickens and fighting roosters as they rushed to the porch whenever anyone came out for some breeze. Auntie Gillie was not pleased. They scratched up her garden patch, and the roosters seemed to have made an arrangement with the clock. They crowed every hour from midnight until six o'clock in the morning and during the day, too. The chickens seemed to know Uncle Tom since he always had rice grains to throw for them.

Every afternoon, Granny Shiela sent me to check whether the chickens had laid. According to her, there was nothing as delicious as a boiled or scrambled egg that was yellow as the sunshine. The hens were not pleased with me interrupting them as they sat in contentment on the eggs they had just laid. Many times I had to run for my life when the hens decided to peck at me or chased me away.

Things soon became rather interesting one day, when I saw a hen clucking and spreading her wings. When I looked closer, there were four little chicks. Instantly I fell in love. I ran to share the good news.

"Auntie Gillie, one of the hens have chicks!" I burst out excitedly. "They are so cute. I feel like cuddling them."

"Good. More eggs for us," Granny Shiela said with a smile.

That was when I realized if we ate the eggs, the hens would not get them to hatch the chicks. From then on I stopped eating the "yard fowl" eggs; after all, I was really killing a new-born chick.

Uncle Tom and the rest of the family couldn't be bothered. "More eggs for me," Alicia said, rolling her eyes. I stopped going to look for the fowl eggs.

One day I saw Uncle Tom sitting in the porch quite preoccupied. Auntie Gillie noticed him too.

"What are you thinking, Tom?" Auntie Gillie asked.

"I noticed there is only one chick left from the set of four that were hatched," Uncle Tom responded. "There must be some rats eating out the baby chicks."

"Or the chicken hawks that are flying around and hiding in the trees," Aunt Gillie said with exasperation.

"Poor chickies," I muttered. Turning to Uncle Tom, I asked, "Can I have one of the chicks as a pet?"

"No," everyone chorused. They could not forget the time I had sneaked a kitten in the house, until the mother came hissing and caterwauling for all its worth as it looked for its offspring.

"Can you imagine a chicken in the house?" Auntie Gillie asked, and Alicia wrinkled her nose.

The next day, the last chick disappeared, and I felt just as unhappy as the mother hen as it rushed around clucking loudly.

"The next time, any one of those hens hatches," Uncle Tom said thoughtfully, "I will take the chickens away and keep them until they get big and can fend for themselves. In that way neither the rats nor the chicken hawks can eat them"

"That's a great idea, Uncle Tom!" I shouted with excitement. "I will help you to look after them How long do we have to wait?."

"Three weeks," Uncle Tom clarified.

I carefully observed Blackie No. 1 (I had given the hens names.) sitting in an old cardboard box. Sure enough some three weeks later, Blackie No. 1 had a brood of six satiny black chicks. They cheeped excitedly and kept close to their mother. I couldn't bear to chase them about. I wanted to observe them, enjoying their sideways movements as they tried to spread their little wings.

I came home from school one day to see a big cardboard box to the side of the porch.

"What's in there?" I asked Granny Shiela.

"Ask your Uncle Tom," she said with a nod of the head.

Uncle Tom revealed that a rat must have eaten three of the chicks, so he decided to keep the others in the box until they were grown. The three of them huddled together to keep warm. Their mother kept patrolling the front of the house squawking angrily as though to say, "Bring my children back to me."

Uncle Tom bought grains for the chicks—starter and grower—and fed them twice each day. I helped as well. Soon they had grown, and then the fighting began in the box.

"There are three cocks in there," Uncle Tom declared. "That's why they are fighting. Old people say, 'Two man rat cyant live in one hole.' Just so with these cocks. I will have to send them to Miss Wendy."

Miss Wendy lived in the countryside, and she reared animals, from goats to pigs to chickens and ducks. The chickens were taken away, and I never saw them again.

I don't think Blackie No. 1 ever forgave Uncle Tom for taking away her chicks, and this is where the story really begins.

The first signs we had that there was another hatch were the soaring chicken hawks circling our property again and again before swooping low over the grass. Uncle Tom stood, legs apart, with a broom stick gripped tightly in his hands.

"I think one of the fowl hatched," he said. "We will have to get the chicks away from her very quickly to protect them from the chicken hawks and the rats."

We soon realised it was Blackie No. 1. She would have nothing to do with Uncle Tom. Every time she saw him, she gave a loud cluck and bustled away with her new brood. This time there were six chicks.

Some afternoons, I returned home from school to see Uncle Tom sitting in the porch, quite preoccupied.

"What's the matter, Uncle Tom?" I asked one afternoon.

"I'm thinking of ways I could get the chicks from the mother hen," he replied. "She too smart for me. If I throw down some rice grains she will come and eat them with her chicks, but the minute I approach, she goes running. I am too old to run behind chickens."

"Well, de best ting you can do, is drunk the modder," Miss Daisie said. She had come for her usual visit and to see what she could get to eat.

"Drunk the mother?" I was puzzled. "What do you mean, Miss Daisie?"

"All Tom has to do is soak rice or pieces of bread in rum and throw it for the fowls to eat. When they fall down drunk, he can go and collect the chicks."

Uncle Tom took Miss Daisie's advice to heart. The next afternoon, when I got home from school, Uncle Tom was in his usual position, looking into the yard at the fowls.

"Did you drunk them, Uncle Tom?" I asked.

Without saying a word, Uncle Tom pointed to a bottle with some punch de crème.

Granny Shiela gave a wheezing laugh. "Dem fowls is some rumbos," she said. "Dey eat de bread and didn't get drunk one bit." I burst out laughing at the image of drunk fowls staggering across our property.

"I will try tomorrow again," Uncle Tom said, determination evident in his voice. "This time I will soak rice in some Guyana El Dorado rum." I didn't take it seriously and went inside to do my usual chores.

Thursday afternoon was rather windy and when I got home, Granny Shiela had retired to her bed. Uncle Tom was once again sitting in the porch. A bottle of rum was on the table next to him.

"I soaked the rice in the rum," he whispered. "Blackie No.1 came with her chicks. I am waiting for her to fall over."

I peeked over the porch and sure enough there were the hens, including Blackie No. 1 and her chicks. Just then a gust of wind came, and to my horror one of the chicks went rolling away.

"Uncle Tom," I said frantically, "the wind blow away the chick." No sooner had the words left my mouth than another chick went rolling across the grass. The chick struggled to its feet but fell over once again.

A closer examination confirmed my horrified shout, "Uncle Tom! You drunk the chicks instead!" Everyone came out of the house in a rush.

"What... what?" Auntie Gillie asked.

"What happen chile?" Granny Shiela asked worriedly.

"She just wants to be noticed," Alicia said, with the usual roll of her eyes.

"Uncle Tom drunk the chicks," I choked out. My eyes were watering.

Auntie Gillie peaked over the porch. "Good God, Tom," she said, "three chicks are lying there."

"I thought the hens were going to eat the rice grains," Uncle Tom said defensively.

"You think they are dead?" I asked in alarm.

"You have to go and get them right now," Auntie Gillie ordered, "or rat, cat or any predator will eat them. We will try to revive them with water."

Uncle Tom gave a huge sigh, got up, and descended the short flight of steps. Four of the five hens and the rooster scattered at his approach, but not Blackie No. 1. Ruffling her feathers, she ran like a bullet towards Uncle Tom. Luckily he had a stick in his hand to shoo her away, or she would have pecked him viciously. She retreated, clucking for all she was worth with the three other chicks.

He gently picked up the three lifeless chicks and brought them into the porch.

"Sue go and look in the kitchen for a box," Auntie Gillie continued to pass orders. "Alicia go in the yard and look for the other three chicks."

"But what if Blackie pick me?" Alicia whined.

"Big girl like yuh frighten fowl?" Granny Shiela said in vexation. "Go fast and come back."

When I returned to the porch with a medium-sized box in my hand, Uncle Tom put the chicks inside. Two were cheeping rather feebly; the other was gasping. Then Auntie Gillie started the water remedy. I gently pried their beaks opened and we dribbled water into their mouths.

Alicia, meanwhile, was hunting in the thick grass. She soon found the other three chicks and brought them in the porch.

"Sue, get some more water." Granny Shiela commanded. "Alicia go back and pull out some grass so dey will be comfortable."

Uncle Tom found a safe place in the corner of the porch. He looked rather ashamed of himself.

I found an old blanket and gently covered the six, gasping chicks.

Just then Miss Daisie turned up, and seeing everyone in the porch, she asked, "What happen now?"

"Uncle Tom drunk the chicks," I burst out. "Now they might all die!" I had tears in my eyes.

"Lawd, Tom," Miss Daisie said. "Yuh cyant follow instructions? I said drunk de fowls, not de chicks."

"How I was to know the chickens would have eaten it?" Uncle Tom tried to defend himself.

Granny Shiela chuckled. "Daisie, we got some rumbo fowls in dis yard. All de fowls eat de rice and not one ah dem fall down."

"The mother hen always scratches the dirt and invites her chicks to eat first," Auntie Gillie clarified. "I think that's why they get drunk in the first place."

"Similar to a human modder, hens always try to provide for and protect der chicks," Miss Daisie advised.

I left the chicks still cheeping feebly that night under the old blanket. When I awoke the next morning and ran toward the box, Auntie Gillie stopped me. "Two of the chicks died," she said.

"Oh no!" I said in sorrow. "Did Uncle Tom bury them? I would have like to be there."

"Oh stop it, Sue," Alicia said in irritation. "They are chickens, not people."

Sometimes, I wished I was big enough to hit Alicia hard.

Uncle Tom came into the house. I turned away from him. I was so angry.

"Look Sue," he tried to explain "if we had left the chicks with their mother, none might have lived. They have a better chance of surviving here. I meant it for good, not bad."

I consoled myself by looking after the four chicks in the box. Every day I fed them and found pleasure in their lively cheeps. But I learned a valuable lesson. This thing called "rum" was dangerous, and even animals could get drunk.

Guided Questions

1. What reason is given for eggs of "yard fowls" being healthier than those from the hatchery?

2. Write down an example in this story where hyperbole is used.

3. In your own words explain what Uncle Tom meant when he said, "Two man rat cyant live in one hole".

4. The narrator gives human qualities to Blackie No. 1. How is this shown?

5. What was the main reason for the rice being soaked in rum?

6. In what way or ways is a mother hen similar to a human being?

Discussion

Why did Sue decide not to eat the yard fowl eggs anymore? Was it a good decision?

Debate who was really to blame for the death of the three chicks.

Suggest another way Uncle Tom could have rescued the chicks.

Discuss what you found sad or amusing about this story.

Vocabulary

Testily

Consoled

Huddled

Chapter Ten

The Pervert

I was either eight or nine when I picked up two bad habits. "Bad words" and eavesdropping became very appealing to me. I would practise repeating expletives I heard from those obnoxious characters in the seediest side of the village when I was in the toilet or the bath, since no one could hear me. Also, big people conversation was very interesting, so as much as possible I loitered about whenever I saw them conversing.

One Saturday afternoon, I had put on a dress I had outgrown when Auntie Gillie brought it to Uncle Tom's attention by saying, "Sue start develop already. She well-shape off, eh? She will have one hell of a behind there." She burst into uproarious laughter.

"What is your conversation Gillie?" Uncle Tom asked irritably. "You have a perverted sense of humour. Why are you looking at the girl's backside?" He looked at me in a guilty manner.

It was the first time I had heard the word "pervert", and I filed it away to use on my friends. The second time I heard the word, Miss Daisie had come over to visit Granny Shiela to talk about—according to Miss Daisie—a "VI" matter, so they went into the dining room and shut the door. Little did Granny Shiela realise that the guava tree was an excellent seat for eavesdropping. I climbed up and took my usual spot. As an excuse for listening to the conversation that was taking place I told myself that if I didn't eavesdrop, I would never learn anything.

"I too vex. I really tink dis man ready to settle down," Granny Shiela began, "I tek me bright self say I gwine cook food fuh he every day."

"Love does mek yuh stupid," Miss Daisie said, shaking her head in commiseration.

"Who tell yuh I love de man," Granny Shiela flared. "I was just doing my Christian and neighbourly duty. I am too old for dem kinda tings." She sounded angry.

"Well," said Miss Daisie. (I was sure she was ticking things off on her fingers.) "Bearing in mind yuh did bake a Valentine Day cake with roses fuh he, instead of he sending anyting fuh you. And bearing in mind, yuh did tek some of yuh pension money and buy one ah dem nice young bwoy shirt fuh he. And bearing in mind, yuh spend de night over by he."

"Hush up," Granny ordered, looking around frantically, "Yuh want people to hear yuh."

I tried to figure out who they were talking about.

"Ole people say, 'dere's no fool like an ole fool'." Miss Daisie sucked her teeth.

"In de first place I am not old," Granny Shiela said with emphasis. "In odder countries, people does reach all seventy-tree and get married."

"You tinking of marrying dat ole pervert?" Miss Daisy sounded scandalized.

"I find you outta place to call Mr. Preddy a pervert," Granny Shiela said angrily. My ears perked. Here was that word again! But Mr. Preddy was a pervert? What did that mean?

Soon, the two best friends were viciously embroiled in a shouting match that brought Auntie Gillie and Uncle Tom running. There, the horrifying tale was revealed! Mr. Preddy had started a relationship with a young girl, and he was three times her age. The gossip mongers said that Gracelyn had shapely long legs and breasts that were shaped like cones.

"That old womaniser!" Auntie Gillie said angrily. "He could be her grandfather."

"True," Granny Shiela's voice sounded miserable and sad. The next time Mr. Preddy came to visit, Granny Shiela took him into the library, and they were locked up in there for a while, their voices rising and falling, indicating a quarrel in full swing. Although I took up my eavesdropping position, I could not hear a thing! Half an hour later, Granny Shiela shouted, "Yuh an ole pervert!"

Mr. Preddy stormed out of the house. His visits diminished, and he walked on the other side of the street whenever he passed by. That was when I realised that old people had relationships like boyfriend and girlfriend. Yikes!

However, it seemed as if the word, "pervert" was a favourite with everybody. I wondered, *when did girls develop 'breast like cones and shapely legs'?* The new knowledge weighed heavily on my mind, but whom could I ask? Alicia and I did not have that kind of relationship, and she would be sure to shut me down. She was such a sourpuss! When I looked at myself in the mirror, all I saw were two pancake-like discs on my chest with a little pointed knob.

My afternoon bath became a ritual of observation and discovery. Contorting my body into various positions, I checked for growth. I measured my waist with the tape measure I had sneaked inside the bathroom; I observed my legs and checked my chest. Uncle Tom would bang on the bathroom door, ordering me to come out.

"Your mother don't send money to pay the water bill," he said irritably. "How much dirt you have so on your skin? Take care, I open this door and drag you out," he threatened.

"Let the girl alone," Aunty Gillie said indulgently. "You don't see she developing?"

But one afternoon, my bathroom rituals were interrupted when I glimpsed a lizard on the bathroom wall, its eyes fastened on my body. The lizard held one position as its tongue flicked in and out, rhythmically.

"Get away," I ordered, sprinkling some water in the lizard's direction. It ran further up the wall before assuming its former position—protruding eyes fixed avidly on my naked body.

I dried my skin hurriedly and went to do my evening chores, but every turn I made, there was the green reptile darting here and there. I wondered whether the lizard was stalking me. Most mornings as I bathed in preparation for school, there was Mr. Lizard perched on the bathroom wall watching intently as I lathered my skin, and in the evening it greeted me in similar fashion. Not only so, but also the family had to chase the lizard away when we sat down to chat in the evenings. In my mind, it had to be the exact same lizard! I could not believe it. I was really being stalked by a reptile!

On a Friday afternoon, some weeks later, Miss Daisie had come over to visit Granny Shiela. Seated in the living room, she sipped a cool drink—a concoction made of lemon and barley—and ate a slice of cassava pone. Their conversation moved from Mr. Preddy's new lady love to speculations of whether she would leave him for a young man, then on to discussing if the African prints sold in Mr. Hardat's haberdashery could be used as curtains.

When I went into the bathroom for my afternoon bath, wonder of wonders, the lizard was not there. I was enjoying my bath tremendously when Uncle Tom banged on the bathroom door. I tried to finish as quickly as possible, but when I pulled my bath towel from the rack, there was the lizard scurrying for the wall. By this time I was so fed up, I gave loud scream.

"This is too much," I muttered to myself. Draped in my towel, I pushed past Uncle Tom and shouted in frustration, "We have a pervert living right here in this house," before bolting for the bedroom. There was a deafening silence. Granny Shiela stammered, "What de girl mean?"

Miss Daisie pursed her lips as though she had smelt a rotten egg. "Ask yuh son-in-law," she muttered, "Is not he been by de batroom door banging."

"What! What!" Granny Shiela's voice trembled with outrage. "Tom," she screamed, "Yuh come here right now."

Uncle Tom came into the room, angry. "I am not a little boy, Shiela," he responded, "nor am I your child."

Immediately Granny Shiela confronted Uncle Tom, "What de ass yuh mean by spying on Sue when she bading?"

"What?" Uncle Tom recoiled in shock, stumbled backwards as he tried to process what Granny Shiela had said.

"Yuh is a nasty pervert," Miss Daisie interjected. "Dat child could be your own daughter. Is nah Gillie say y'all gwine adopt de child?" She posed the question to Granny Shiela who was clenching and unclenching her fists.

Unaware of the chaos I had created, I dried my skin and put on my clean clothes. I was ready to tell Granny Shiela about this perverted, inquisitive creature who was making my life a misery.

When I entered the living room, I discovered Auntie Gillie, Uncle Tom, Granny Shiela and Miss Daisie involved in a vicious quarrel. Uncle Tom was red in the face, and Auntie Gillie was crying her heart out.

"If it means I have to divorce you, Tom, I will," Auntie Gillie blubbered.

"What happen Auntie Gillie?" I asked in bewilderment. I thought Uncle Tom and Auntie Gillie had a happy marriage.

"How yuh mean what happen?" Miss Daisie bawled out, "Is not you say a pervert living here after yuh Uncle Tom was by de batroom door?"

Granny Shiela looked as though she was having a heart attack. "Gillie, is what kinda man yuh bring inna my house?" She was gasping for breath!

Auntie Gillie wailed loudly while Uncle Tom sat with his hands on his head.

"Uncle Tom is a pervert?" I asked in confusion.

"Is not dat yuh say?" Miss Daisie jumped up, beside herself with rage.

"I didn't say that!" I denied, shaking my head vigorously. "I was talking 'bout the lizard."

"LIZARD!" The voices of the three women rose to a crescendo.

"Yes," I tried to explain. "I never accused Uncle Tom of anything."

Granny Shiela's head swivelled to face Miss Daisie who moved back a step. Granny's anger had found a new outlet.

"Yuh is a wicked woman," she said hoarsely. "How dare yuh accuse my son-in-law of such a ting?" Her anger was palatable.

"But I... I... I... is not dat she say?" stuttered Miss Daisie.

"Yuh have a devious, evil mind, too much vice," Granny Shiela interrupted. "Get outta me house."

Miss Daisie turned and quickly left the room. "And doan bodder to call me when yuh have yuh troubles," was her parting remark. I stood rooted to the spot while Uncle Tom sat as still as a statue with his face still buried in his hands. I couldn't believe all this occurred because I used the word "pervert".

"Yuh come here young lady," Granny Shiela said. I shuffled forward until I stood in front of Granny Shiela.

"Sumitra, if I put my hand on yuh, I kill yuh dead," Granny Shiela said fiercely. "Where yuh hear de word 'pervert'?

"You and Miss Daisie was talking bout Mr. Preddy," I confessed shamefacedly. "Then Auntie Gillie told her friend Linda bout it."

"All you does talk too much slackness," At last Uncle Tom found his voice as he confronted both women. "Is the two of you she hear talking. All you does do in y'all spare time is mind other people business."

Auntie Gillie didn't say a word.

Not so with Granny Shiela. Fuming with righteous indignation, she ordered Uncle Tom, "Cut she backside."

"Me ain't touching she," Uncle Tom said, "and I tell you already I am not a child." Then he stormed out of the house.

It was left to Auntie Gillie to administer the punishment. She plied the belt furiously, crying as she did so, while my screams intermingled with Granny Shiela's bellows.

By the time Auntie Gillie was finished, she was panting in exhaustion as if she had run a marathon.

"You must learn to stop eavesdropping and keep your mouth shut," she said, "I hope you learn your lesson,"

I didn't say "bip or bap" as I rubbed my smarting behind. I slunk into the bedroom, fuming with anger and muttering words under my breath to conjure up fire and brimstones. I wanted so badly to use one of the vilest expletives I had overheard but was afraid lightning would strike me dead. Alicia, in the meantime, had bypassed the sitting room and headed for the bedroom. She had heard everything and was chortling with delight over my fall from grace.

"Oh Pervert! Dear Pervert!" Alicia sang in a falsetto voice.

I folded in my lips and waited until Alicia was fast asleep, then let out the loudest fart I could, before I dived into bed. I felt some satisfaction when Alicia jumped up with fright.

" Wha... what?" Alicia asked looking around wide-eyed.

I simply pretended to snore and wiggled into the most comfortable position I could, given the circumstances. I was doubly pleased when the smell lit up the room and Alicia gagged horribly before bolting out.

"All of you is wicked people," I muttered crossly before willing myself to sleep.

By the next morning Granny Shiela had cooled down. She made some eggnog, lemony pancakes, bacon, eggs and garlic bread for Uncle Tom's breakfast as an apology, but she kept muttering to herself about 'upstarted children' and 'nosy neighbours'. Alicia was allowed to partake of the lavish breakfast, while I was only given two slices of garlic bread.

As though satisfied with the confusion it had made, the lizard was nowhere to be seen when I went for my bath that afternoon. Later when Auntie Gillie and Uncle Tom had gone on a peace-making date at the Hunan Gardens restaurant, I approached Granny Shiela who was sitting in the rocking chair. Her right hand supported her chin, as she stared into space.

"I am sorry, Granny Shiela," I said remorsefully, "I didn't mean to make any trouble, but the lizard...."

Granny Shiela gave a small start, then sighed heavily. "I had time to tink about it. Yuh know ole people say dat lizards are reincarnation of fast, inquisitive, people."

"What is reincarnation, Granny Shiela?" I asked.

"Go and research it." This was her usual response whenever she didn't want to get into the technical details of a word. "But I will have to wipe out dis place wid blue and white lavender and put some sticky glue by de window of de batroom. Dat should keep dem away."

For months, Miss Daisie held Granny Shiela malice until Easter Sunday, when they became fast friends again. I decided there and then I would try my very best to stop eavesdropping!

Guided Questions

1. What are two themes brought out in this story?

2. What does the abbreviation VI mean?

3. Who is a pervert?

4. What figure of speech is associated with this phrase "exact same lizard"? What is the purpose of using this phrase? Identify another example of this figure of speech.

5. What evidence is there in this chapter to show that Granny Shiela and Miss Daisie are best friends?

6. Uncle Tom was accused of being a pervert. Who is really responsible for blaming him? Justify your answer.

7. How did Granny Shiela show Uncle Tom she was sorry for misjudging him?

8. How did Auntie Gillie show Uncle Tom she was sorry for misjudging him?

9. "I stood rooted to the spot while Uncle Tom sat as still as a statue". What two figures of speech are used here?

10. Why do you think there was not a good relationship between Alicia and Sue? What evidence is there in the chapter to support your answer?

Discussion

Do you think Granny Shiela is too old to be in love? At what age do you think a woman/man should fall in love? Why do you think so?

Do you think Sue deserved the whipping?

Do you think Granny Shiela should have made a verbal apology to Uncle Tom? Why or why not?

Which other animals/insects show human qualities?

Word Bank

You have encountered some new words to add to your vocabulary. Use a dictionary to find the meaning and use them in sentences for practice.

<table>
<tr><td>uproarious</td><td>administer</td></tr>
<tr><td>inconspicuous</td><td>slunk</td></tr>
<tr><td>frantically</td><td>conjure</td></tr>
<tr><td>embroiled</td><td>chortling</td></tr>
<tr><td>avidly</td><td>falsetto</td></tr>
<tr><td>lathered</td><td>lavish</td></tr>
<tr><td>indignation</td><td>remorsefully</td></tr>
<tr><td>expletive</td><td>obnoxious</td></tr>
<tr><td>speculation</td><td>rhythmically</td></tr>
<tr><td>chaos</td><td>protruding</td></tr>
<tr><td>bewilderment</td><td>commiserate</td></tr>
<tr><td>reincarnation</td><td>palatable</td></tr>
<tr><td>vigorously</td><td>crescendo</td></tr>
<tr><td>devious</td><td></td></tr>
</table>

Activity

Use these words and the rest of words you have been compiling to have a spelling and vocabulary competition.

Chapter Eleven

Easter Misadventure

Auntie Gillie had invited her best friend, Miss Harper, to spend the Easter with us. She had a son, Charlie, who was very irritating. He attended the same school as I and looked at everything as a competition between us. I had become involved in all kinds of boys sports—from playing cricket in the road to rolling the rim of a bicycle wheel with just a piece of stick to guide its movements. I also played football with the school's team because it was a mixed team, and although the boys just tolerated me, I didn't mind.

Every turn I made, Charlie was, according to Granny Shiela, "foot and foot behind yuh". And he talked non-stop. I wondered if he talked in his sleep. I used to breathe a sigh of relief when he went for his afternoon naps since, according to his mother, "Sleep allows children to grow". To my mind, it was clearly untrue since I didn't sleep much during the day, and I was taller than him.

Miss Harper babied Charlie so much. I understood, then, why he behaved the way he did at school. He was short and slender and looked as though a puff of wind would blow him away. According to Granny Shiela, "Yuh doan see he is wind spirit? Is de wind does blow he to de front a de race." In essence it was true because he did fairly well at our primary school sports and made sure no one forgot about it.

"He's wind spirit," Uncle Tom muttered softly after Charlie went on and on about his performance at the inter-school sports, while his mother sat smiling for all she was worth and nodding like a puppet.

Granny Shiela interrupted, "Miss Harper yuh must give dis boy yam and plantain. He too bony, man. Look at Sue, she same age wid him and could eat soup on he head."

"Well," Miss Harper replied. I could see she was displeased with the comment Granny Shiela made. "Our family are not built like giants, but we are smart and swift."

Because I knew our school's football team had won the inter-school championship for three years in a row, I didn't feel bad that Charlie boasted about his ability to do well at track and field. I knew I could outrun him on a football field any time. Football was a game that called for far more stamina than running a hundred metre dash.

I knew Easter Saturday would not be the best day for me. There were two reasons! One: I had to tolerate two of the most irritating persons! Two: Auntie Gillie decided to have Alicia and me join her in the kitchen to see how hot cross buns were made. Each of us had to make a batch of six. Charlie stood by making all sorts of silly comments. I itched to throw some flour in his face.

My hands were a little heavy with the flour, so my cross buns came out very stiff. Alicia's cross buns were light and tasty. Granny Shiela was quick to praise her after one bite. "Yuh will make a good cook," she said to Alicia, then turning to me, she added, "Yuh need to take some time from dem books you keep reading, running 'bout de yard like a wild horse, and learn to do tings in de kitchen. Yuh is a girl, not a boy!"

Alicia and Charlie looked at each other and burst out laughing. In my heart I vowed to make them pay.

School was on vacation, so we were allowed a little freedom to go for an afternoon walk to the playing field. Children from our school went there to play as well. Since Guyana is so flat, we learnt at school that our country was below water levels and prone to flooding. One thing that was a bit offsetting about the playing field was the canal surrounding it. We were cautioned to always play in the middle of the field.

Auntie Gillie and Miss Harper had bought three kites and told us we could try them out in the pasture. I was very happy with the kite Auntie Gillie bought. It had several geometry-shaped ribbons at the side. When I looked carefully, I could see the picture of a young girl.

Without hesitation, I quickly got ready, picked up my kite and waited impatiently for the two turtles to join me.

"Alicia, as the oldest, you are to keep an eye on Sue and Charlie," Auntie Gillie warned.

"Yes, Auntie Gillie," Alicia muttered. She didn't appreciate hanging out with me.

The playing field was crowded. I saw some friends from my football team. Someone had walked with a ball, and we soon organized to play against members of a team from another school. They, too, were enjoying the freedom of the holidays by playing on the field. I was already dressed in my shorts and sneakers, so it wasn't a problem warming up. It did not matter to me that I was the only girl playing in the game.

"Why can't you give up your tomboyish ways?" Alicia asked with a curl of her lips. "We came to fly kites, not to get into trouble."

"How can I get into trouble by just playing a friendly football game?" I argued

"I forbid you from paying football," Alicia ordered. "Auntie Gillie said I was in charge."

Ignoring Alicia, I shoved my kite into Charlie's hands. "Hold this. I won't be long," I said and rushed away.

I knew that Alicia was fuming because I did not obey her, but I couldn't be bothered. I was out to enjoy myself.

The football match was exhilarating, and I was totally enjoying myself when I felt someone grab me by my jersey. I thought one of the other players was trying to tackle me, so I gave a back kick. Someone screamed. It sounded familiar. When I spun around, there was Alicia rolling on the ground, in tears and holding her right knee. Apparently, she had come to forcibly stop me from playing the "boys" game.

"What happened to you?" I asked the obvious.

"You kicked me. I am going to tell Auntie Gillie," she blubbered. My heart sank.

"I didn't know it was you," I tried to explain.

A section of the team came around including the coach. I don't know where he came from, but he checked out Alicia's knees and helped her to her feet. She was milking his sympathy for all she was worth.

"I was only trying to tell her that Charlie lost her kite." Alicia shoulders heaved but there was no tear in her eyes.

"What?" I hollered. "How you mean Charlie lost my kite?"

Just then Charlie came running up. "Your string cut way," he said breathlessly. "The kite went into the canal."

I never told him to fly my kite. I just told him to hold it, but I saw when he sneaked a glance at Alicia. My thoughts immediately went into analytical mode, *They deliberately planned to destroy my kite, but I'll get even.*

The other members of the football team slapped me on the back. "Flying kites is girls' stuff," the captain said. "Let's continue the game."

"Why don't we invite Charlie to play with us?" I asked. "He's a good footballer too."

Charlie looked super proud and immediately began to play aggressively. Whenever I had the ball, he was sure to tackle me. I waited for my chance. I dribbled the ball with skill and headed to the far end of the pasture. The older players saw Charlie pursuing me and thought he was going to get the ball away so play could resume. The young players like me were running for all they were worth to catch up with us. When I got the end of the pasture, just at the edge of canal, I feigned to the left. Charlie couldn't stop his plunge into the canal. He screamed like a girl as he floundered about.

The other players came barrelling across the pasture, including Alicia, who stood wringing her hands. They formed a human chain and quickly pulled Charlie out. He was blubbering with fright. Alicia tried to pat him down, while I looked shocked at his misadventure.

"He was running really fast," I said. "He couldn't stop himself."

That was the end of the football game since Charlie was wet and had begun to shiver. The three of us headed home without any conversation. Auntie Gillie was horrified at my dishevelment. I had lost my hair ribbons, and my clothes were dusty. Miss Harper gave a gasp of horror at the sight of her wet and shivering son.

"Yuh are de oldest here, Alicia," Granny Shiela said in annoyance. "Yuh couldn't make sure de two younger children keep out of trouble?"

"It's Sue's fault," Alicia tried to defend herself. "She went to play football with the boys in the field."

"Me?" I opened my eyes wide with pretended shock. "I only played football because you and Charlie lost my kite."

"Lost the kite," Auntie Gillie said in disbelief. "How?

"I don't know," I responded. "I asked Charlie to hold it for me."

"So where are the other kites?" Uncle Tom asked.

No one responded. In the confusion, we had forgotten all about them.

Miss Harper whisked Charlie away for a hot bath. Alicia received a stern lecture on being responsible and I was reminded once again I was a girl and not a boy. One of the things I learnt about me is I had a mean streak and I liked to get even; but I consoled myself that if I didn't people would take advantage of me.

Guided Questions

1. Identify a theme explored in this story.

2. There are two settings mentioned in this story. Explain what activity takes place in each setting.

3. Explain how the narrator does not fit into the role expected of her.

4. In two short paragraphs describe the relationship between the narrator and (a) Charlie (b) Alicia. Use evidence from this chapter to support your answer.

Discussion

Why does Miss Harper say that sleep allows children to grow? Is this true?

How would you describe Miss Harper as a parent?

Vocabulary

Exhilarating

Analytical

Floundered

Chapter Twelve

Superstitious Beliefs!

After my Easter experience, I didn't know who or what I wanted to be. I didn't want to be called a tomboy all the time; but I was also afraid of becoming too girlie. I mostly kept to myself, grouching at how boring my village had become, when suddenly I discovered that the village matriarchs, the teenagers, and even the older men were all atwitter. The "big screen" cinema was coming to Golden Grove. (Persons who had been exposed to life in town spoke always about the big screen to describe their "cinema" experience.) There were two cinemas in town—the Strand and the Globe, but it was the Lyric cinema that was being built, right there in the heart of the village.

Everyone had their say about the matter.

"This cinema ting gwine mek de young people stop gwine church," Mrs. King said angrily. "Let de cinema stay in town."

"Dese young people doan realise dat is de devil does put de ideas in dese people head to make de pictures. Soon they gwine start practising it." As Miss Forde made this announcement, she wagged her finger.

"Why yuh doan shut yuh mout," a young man called out. "De young people in de village ain't got nottin' to do and nowhere to go. Is not alyuh same ole people does say idleness is de devil's tool. Dis will keep us outta trouble.'

The argument waged back and forth. The younger people were eager for the pictures to start showing, while the older ones listened to the ongoing argument with trepidation, thinking that God would rain fire and brimstone on the village for dabbling in things that would turn the young people away from church.

The deciding factor came when the owner visited Golden Grove. He had a thick cigar clenched tightly between his teeth, and his hands clasped behind his back. He stood surveying the men at work on the new cinema and said, "We need more manpower. Where is the contractor?"

The contractor, Mr. Crandon, came hastily. It was comical to see this tall man being very submissive to the short, pudgy man who owned the theatre. "Yes, Boss man," he answered in a respectful manner.

"See if you can employ another 50 men," he ordered. "I want this cinema to be finished for the August vacation. The kids need somewhere to go."

When the older women of the village realized their husbands and sons would obtain jobs to help the finances of the family, they quickly changed their minds about the new cinema.

Miss Daisie got involved when Mr. Crandon offered a job to her godson, Godson. I knew Godson since he always visited Miss Daisie on weekends so his mother could "ketch she breath" according to Miss Daisie.

Godson was as thin as a broomstick. No matter how much he ate, it seemed as though his stomach was a cavern because no one could see where the food went. Uncle Tom said he had "bad worms". Nevertheless, he had a pleasant personality and a grin that was like a ray of sunshine on a rainy day. The villagers could call on Godson to run any errand for them, and he did so without making a fuss.

"You tink is easy to have tree children in four years?" Miss Daisie asked Granny Shiela, while Aunty Gillie sat in the corner reading a book. "De boy is de middle chile. And de last girl only have to roll up she big eyes and full it with water for the modder to neglect de boy."

"Yes," agreed Granny Shiela. "I hear he used to beat his head on de ground to make his modder notice him." She shook her head sadly.

"Dat is why de boy can't learn," Miss Daisie responded. "His head get too hard from all de beating it get."

"Are you saying is that he is not mentally sound," I interrupted. I had read that phrase two weeks ago and had eagerly awaited an opportunity to use it.

"Lost his marbles, if you ask me," Alicia muttered. We burst into laughter simultaneously.

"I heard bot' of yuh!" Auntie Gillie said sharply. "Don't talk 'bout de less fortunate dat way." I felt rather embarrassed at my unkind remarks and muttered "sorry" under my breath. Alicia stayed silent.

The two older women were quiet for a while before Miss Daisie said, "He too young to work in dat den of iniquity. He only tirteen years. I dunno what wrong wid he modder." She sucked her teeth and sighed.

The cinema progressed with enormous speed and we all waited with bated breath for it to be completed. It was going to show movies straight out of India and China. Everyone had heard of the movie "Indiana Jones" and the men who had seen it in at the city's cinema declared it was the "baddest thing ever". I hoped Auntie Gillie would allow us to go.

Godson still came to visit Miss Daisie on weekends. The money he made working on the cinema helped his mother tremendously. Even Miss Daisie benefited as he would give her a little "small change" now and then. The men took advantage of Godson's easy-going nature and his willingness to help and sent him out on all kinds of errands.

Things were going smoothly, so it was quite a surprise that Saturday afternoon when I heard a loud caterwauling coming toward our yard. As I peeped out the window, I saw Miss Daisie with her hands on her head moving as fast as she could.

"Granny Shiela, Miss Daisie is bawling," I reported.

"I wonder what wrong wid she now," Granny Shiela said irritably. "Go sprinkle some salt in front de door quick, before she bring she trials and crosses in here." I scampered to obey before I let in Miss Daisie.

"O Gawd, Miss Shiela, Godson done gone and dead!" Miss Daisie came through the door like a whirlwind. She was shaking uncontrollably.

"What?" Granny Shiela's eyes opened wide. "When? How?" she sputtered to a stop.

"He fall off de roof of de cinema and break he neck." Miss Daisie wheezed out.

"Jesus Christ!" Granny Shiela said hoarsely, before making the sign of the cross, looking up into the sky and saying as piously as possible, "Father forgive me for taking yuh Son's name in vain."

"Dem men send Godson up dere because he de youngest among dem. Just because he ain't too bright, dem take advantage of he. O God! Meh godson, Godson, dead!" Miss Daisie wailed, putting her hands on her head again

Auntie Gillie came around to see what the noise was about. She hugged Miss Daisie tightly murmuring, "Don't take on so Miss Daisie. You will get sick. Let me bring some golden apple juice to cool you down. I made a nice sweet potato pudding too," Auntie Gillie coaxed.

I went for a towel, as commanded by Granny Shiela, and Miss Daisie wiped her face before draining the glass of golden apple juice and asking for another.

"But Shiela," Miss Daisie said after a while, "I shudda realise something bad was goin' happen. Remember I tell you my left eye was jumping fuh two weeks now?"

"True," Granny Shiela said rocking back and forth in her chair. "When yuh left eye start to twitch, it means some bad luck or sometin' bad gwine happen to yuh or yuh family."

"And just two nights ago I went by Hoo Ching to buy a chicken fry rice, and a black cat come out from nowhere and run in front of me." Miss Daisie continued.

"Why yuh didn't turn back?" Granny Shiela demanded. "Yuh doan play wid black cats, 'specially at nights. Dat was a evil spirit walking 'bout."

"Ah was too hungry," Miss Daisie admitted shamefacedly.

"You are always hungry," I thought to myself as my eyes met Alicia's.

"It must be follow yuh home. Yuh went in de house backward?" Granny Shiela asked. "You make a cross wid yuh two shoes in front de door?"

"No," Miss Daisie admitted in sorrow. "Godson did spend de weekend wid me and was waiting on de food."

"De jumby ketch he cos he was de youngest one dere," Granny Shiela spoke with authority.

There was silence for a while as the three women sat ruminating on all the little clues that should have alerted them that something bad would happen.

I sat shaking my head in bewilderment, for I could not process that Godson was dead.

"De owl been hooting up a storm in de air," Granny Shiela finally said. "I just start pleading de blood ah Jesus. I say it seven times. I walk from window to window and door to door."

"And the dogs were howling all night last night," Alicia interjected with a shiver. I stared at her in shock. This was the first time I realized that she could be frightened too.

"They eder see a spirit, or warning yuh somebody gwine dead," Granny Shiela said.

Miss Daisie shook her head sorrowfully.

"I had a weird dream too," Auntie Gillie said suddenly, startling me. "I dream that Godson mother get another baby and it was a boy."

"When you dream 'bout marriage is funeral and when you dream 'bout birt' is deat'," Granny Shiela said, nodding her head as though it were written in stone.

"I gotta go an visit Godson modder and help her to organize," Miss Daisie said, lumbering to her feet. "I will see yuh all tomorrow."

As soon as Miss Daisie left, Granny Shiela became busy. "Sue go in de kitchen and you gwine see de small jar wid de blue. Bring one right now. Gillie go in de medicine chest and bring de small bottle of white lavender oil."

"Which blue, Granny Shiela?" I asked in confusion.

"De one I does use wid de white clothes," she answered irritably.

Granny Shiela set all of us to mopping and cleaning the entire house that afternoon, for as she said, "Just in case Daisie bring she bad luck over here or de jumby follow she". She placed a pair of shoes in the sign of a cross in front of the two doors for double protection against any evil spirit that wanted to enter. I was never so scared in my life. I never knew young people could die! I felt really ashamed of the many times we had spoken unkindly about Godson. I wondered how his mother would make out now he was dead. For many nights, I would wake up to listen for the hooting owl or the howling dogs. If I heard any, I would make the sign of the cross and pray myself to sleep.

When we went to the funeral, Granny Daisie made sure I had a nail in my little bag, while Auntie Gillie had three pegs of garlic in her purse. I don't know what Granny Shiela gave Alicia and she never said what she carried, but for one week after the funeral, she told me to tell Miss Daisie that she was sleeping whenever she came to visit.

As for Godson's mother? She got paid a sum of money from the boss man and the cinema opened in time for the August holidays. The first time the young boys saw "Tarzan of the Apes" on the big screen, some ran out of the cinema, while others hid under the benches. They really thought the tiger would jump out of the screen and eat them. The old biddies who were against the cinema in the first place, went to view a movie now and then. Afterword, they would congregate to discuss how much they enjoyed the "pickcha".

The exposure of the villagers to the house telephone began another talking point in the village. Only those who were a little "well-off" could afford it. I guess we must have been in that category. It came with a long black cord that allowed Granny Shiela to conduct her conversations from the porch where everyone could see and hear her and know the Forde's family had bought a telephone. Other families followed suit, and cinema life gradually became associated with "special occasions" or for the "courting young people". Superstitious beliefs, too, had taken a "back seat", but they surfaced every now and then.

Guided Questions

1. State the characters who were mainly affected by the events in this story. Give reasons for your answer.

2. What is the major theme in this story?

3. Identify one instance in this chapter where a superstitious action was practiced by Granny Shiela.

4. Compare the responses of the older generation to having a cinema in the village with that of the younger generation.

5. What changed the minds of the older generation towards the new cinema?

6. A new figure of speech used in the story is "euphemism". Find out what it is and identify an example used in the chapter.

7. Find one piece of evidence in this chapter that indicates people's respect for God.

8. What two other words can be use instead of "jumby"?

9. Briefly explain what lessons the narrator learned from the events in this story.

Discussion

Why are cinemas no longer patronized as before?

Are there any traditional superstitious practices your parents or grand-parents do?

Do you think superstition still influences our beliefs or actions? Explain.

Chapter Thirteen

Wedding Watchers and Wedding Crashers

Miss Daisie was in her elements. Her half-brother granddaughter was getting married to a young man that she had been seeing for the past seven years.

"Is time he put de ring on she finger," Miss Daisie told Granny Shiela. "Dem courting since dey was going to primary school. Yuh think is two licks Petra get fuh dat boy! I tell yuh. I really glad fuh dem."

"Where are they going to have the wedding, Miss Daisie?" Auntie Gillie asked.

"I tink is de Presbyterian Church in Langley Park," Miss Daisie responded, "but dey still finalizing ting."

From all accounts, it was going to be a small wedding. The young man, Burton, who was a postal worker did not receive a big salary and Petra was a preschool teacher, so her salary was minimal as well. She had been thinking of opening her own preschool since she received training in "Teaching the Young Child" at the Skills and Arts Alternative College. Their combined salary would enable them to make plans for buying their own home and starting their family.

Miss Daisie continued her running commentary about the wedding every time she came to visit Granny Shiela. "Dey decide to invite forty people, including de people from de church and her immediate family. I tell she I have a good friend I have to invite." Miss Daisie nodded her head emphatically.

"Who you talking 'bout Miss Daisie?" I asked.

"Yuh have to ask dat?" Miss Daisie said dismissively. "Everybody know yuh grandmodder is me best friend. De whole family is invited to de wedding."

The thought of being invited to the wedding excited me since it was the first time I was going to attend one. I wondered if Auntie Gillie would buy me a new dress.

"What are you giving them for a present?" I asked Miss Daisie.

"My presence," Miss Daisie responded. "What more do dey need?"

Auntie Gillie decided she would buy the newly-weds an electric kettle. She could not bear the idea of attending a wedding empty-handed.

The wedding reception was to be held from 4:30 p.m. at the Golden Grove Community Centre. Granny Shiela was pleased.

"I doan like dese far driving," Granny Shiela said, "Memba dat is in de countryside. First ting, place black like pitch and de mosquitoes bigger dan two donkeys tied togedder."

Uncle Tom remarked, "Gillie, wedding does have bare confusion. I don't know if I want to go."

"You can't do Daisie dat," Granny Shiela argued. "And I already have a real nice dress I want to wear."

Uncle Tom was still not comfortable about the word-of-mouth invitation. According to Auntie Gillie weddings attracted two kinds of crowds—the wedding crashers and the wedding watchers. When I asked her to explain the two terms, Auntie Gillie said, "The wedding crashers are the people who turn up uninvited by the bridal party." She gave a chuckle before she continued. "The wedding watchers are those persons who religiously congregate outside the church wherever a wedding takes place. They are the unofficial commentators on the attire that is worn. They take note of whose dresses are too long or too short, the outdated fashions and those persons whom they just know had rented an outfit for the occasion."

"Sometimes the crowd is so thick, you have to walk around them," Uncle Tom added. "One time, Miss Jordan saw the wife of Principal Thomas going into the church. One of the teachers had gotten married. She called out for everyone to hear, 'Eh eh! Like Miss Thomas only have one good dress. Is not the same dress, she wear last month to Linksy wedding?' Mrs. Thomas was so embarrassed that she waited till the crowd had dispersed before she came out the church."

Auntie Gillie gave a chuckle. "Tom, you remember when Labba daughter-in-law shout out to the well-dressed woman who had obviously come from abroad that she had a dress just like that at home?"

Auntie Gillie continued to reminisce. "The woman's voice was loud so everyone heard when she said, 'You can't even go where I got this dress. However, if you like it so much, I'll leave it with Mrs. Wilshire for you when I return to Paris.' Labba daughter-in-law felt so embarrassed, she tried to explain to all who were willing to listen that she had the same dress. Imagine when she wore the dress to church the next Sunday, some malicious person had already spread the rumour that a wedding guest had left the dress for Labba daughter-in-law. From that day, people forget her first name was Belinda and started calling her Broddough."

Everyone burst into uproarious laughter before Uncle Tom once again shared his misgivings about attending the wedding, but Auntie Gillie was adamant we should attend.

Miss Daisie seemed more excited about the wedding than the bride and groom because every opportunity she got, she engaged in conversation about the momentous occasion and mentioned the lovely dress she had bought and planned to wear.

"How many people have been invited, Miss Daisie?" Auntie Gillie asked.

"Well, de young people say dey only catering for sixty," Miss Daisie replied. "Yuh know de real married life start after de wedding, so dey have to save deir money for dat"

I could not understand how Miss Daisie, who had never been married, could speak with such authority.

"Ah wonder if Daisie realise de number of people invited going up and up," Granny Shiela told Auntie Gillie. "I hope dey have enough food to feed de people an dem."

"The two ah dem done plan everyting," Miss Daisie told Granny Shiela, "The wedding should go smooth smooth." I wondered if they knew that Miss Daisie had taken the liberty to invite other people.

In Golden Grove where people operated like one big family, the discussion about a wedding was, in effect, an unspoken invitation to crash—especially with Miss Daisie speaking about the range of mouth-watering delights.

Three weeks before the wedding Burton heard a conversation that went like this, "I already buy a nice shirt. Bwai Daisie say food and drink like joke. I gwine to be dere fuh true."

Hearing the name Daisie, Burton put "two and two together", realizing the man was speaking about his wedding. When he turned around and looked at the man making the plans, he had never seen the man before. That was when Burton realised there was every likelihood wedding crashers were planning to attend his wedding. He went to his wife-to-be.

"Petra. Like Miss Daisie inviting the whole of Golden Grove. I am not a rich man. And beside I thought we say we only inviting sixty people." Burton was rather upset.

Petra sucked her teeth loudly. "These people too lickerish."

"I think the best thing to do is to have a list with all the names of the people who we invite, and the people whose names not on the list cannot come into the reception hall."

Burton got his friend Constable Andrews to man the door of the reception hall.

The day of the wedding finally came and so, too, did the wedding watchers and crashers. Three months before the wedding, Uncle Tom had bought a second-hand car and spent most of his evenings cleaning it and checking to make sure it worked well. We dressed to reflect that we were not hand-to-mouth and were especially pleased we would be driving through the village for everyone to see us. That would certainly give the wedding watchers something to talk about!

Granny Shiela had on a yellow dress with splashes of green. Auntie Gillie pressed Alicia's hair, and Alicia wore a lovely light pink sheath and a pair of high-heeled shoes. She had not yet mastered the art of walking far distances with high-heeled shoes. I found it hilarious when she wobbled across the room trying to find her balance. After she had almost twisted her ankle, Auntie Gillie placed the high-heeled shoes in the cupboard. I was not allowed to press my hair; its thickness was contained with two broad blue ribbons to match the colour of my dress that came just below my knees. I don't know why Auntie Gillie gave me a pair of white stockings to wear with my black shoes. I thought I looked like a clown. Auntie Gillie was dressed in a gold dress with sequins that glittered. Her up-swept hairstyle was fashionable. Uncle Tom looked dapper in his brown suit.

Miss Daisie had begged for a ride, claiming she did not want to walk the long distance to the Community Centre.

"Ah doan want to be sweaty," she explained. Uncle Tom could not refuse her; after all, she had invited us to the wedding.

By four o'clock, everyone was dressed and ready but there was no sign of Miss Daisie. Uncle Tom, being a stickler for punctuality, began to fret. "If it's one thing I don't appreciate is arriving at a function late and having everybody staring at me," he said testily.

When Miss Daisie arrived at 4:45 p.m. huffing and puffing, my jaw dropped open in shock. Miss Daisie had somehow squeezed herself into a red dress with white ribbons around the neck and sleeves. I could see the bulges all around. It certainly was not appropriate for a woman of her age. Alicia's eyes met mine across the room. It was the first time we agreed about something even though we didn't say a word. Alicia tried to keep a straight face, and I began coughing loudly to camouflage my laughter.

Without missing a beat, Uncle Tom said, "Let's go. We are late."

Auntie Gillie placed the wedding present in the trunk of the car, and Uncle Tom herded us into the vehicle. Auntie Gillie sat in the front passenger seat, while the four of us squeezed into the back seat with Alicia and I squashed in the middle between Granny Shiela and Miss Daisie. The car wheezed and groaned, before it lurched into motion. I prayed that it would not break down before we got to our destination. Uncle Tom had only driven it twice up and down our street.

It was the loud voices that alerted me that we had arrived. The thick crowd swarmed around the door that was slightly ajar. Some of the wedding watchers pointed out persons they knew, while other watched with envious eyes.

"I reach here first," a man dressed in a light blue suit was arguing as he pushed against door of the community centre.

"You pushed your way in," another man declared, grabbing the "blue" man by his collar.

"Where is your invitation?" shouted Constable Andrews.

Feeling rather important, Miss Daisie squeezed out the car, shouting to the top of her voice, "I am family. Let me tru." Uncle Tom followed gingerly in her wake.

Not surprisingly, no one heard her and with everyone pushing forward, she fell down, letting out a gut-wrenching bellow. Auntie Gillie was in the process of opening the front door of the car. She froze. The crowd went quiet. The constable closed the door of the reception hall with a decisive slam. Granny Shiela had gotten out of the car, and stood by the back door with both hands covering her ears. Alicia and I, who had not come out of the car huddled together in dismay.

Uncle Tom did an about turn, like a military sergeant in a parade, and headed towards the car. "You see why I didn't want to come to this wedding in the first place," he said stating the obvious. "Gillie, tell your mother to get back in the car or I am leaving her right here." Granny Shiela squeezed back in the car immediately.

Without another word, Uncle Tom drove away. There was silence in the car as it sped towards home until Alicia bravely said, "Uncle Tom I am hungry. We are not getting anything to eat tonight?"

Uncle Tom did not answer. Then Auntie Gillie said, "Tom I did not cook today because I thought we were going to have food at the wedding. The children are hungry." Uncle Tom kept driving.

When he finally stopped, I read the sign below the flashing lights. It read "Ching Wah Oriental Foods". Still in silence, Uncle Tom got out and went into the restaurant, bypassing the line of customers that snaked out onto the road. He came out in less than ten minutes with five paper bags in his hands. I guess he was given royal treatment because of the way he was dressed.

Uncle Tom unceremoniously pushed a bag into the hands of each of us and drove towards home. For once, Granny Shiela did not engage anyone in conversation. As soon as we arrived, she ate half of her fried rice and put the rest into the fridge. So did everyone else. The look on Uncle Tom's face made us all afraid to mention Miss Daisie's name.

For two days, everyone walked on eggshells around Uncle Tom; Miss Daisie was scarce as good gold. It was the Monday newspapers, however, that brought things to a head like a festering abscess.

Mr. Preddy passed by brandishing the newspaper in his hand. "Shiela, I see yuh best friend and son-in-law make de news." There in the front page was a grainy picture of Miss Daisie on the ground surrounded by a horde of people while Uncle Tom seemed to be fleeing the scene.

Apparently, a news reporter from the "Glover Newspaper" was looking for a front page story. The wedding watchers gave him all the relevant information about the melee, and he was able to turn the melee into a newsworthy event. Just below the teaser was the headline: Wedding Crashers. "Rampant hunger forces wedding guests to fight for a chance to eat."

Uncle Tom ranted and raged and promised to sue the newspaper. Auntie Gillie moaned about the indignity of people associating her with "fighting for food".

"Auntie Gillie, did we get an invitation?" I asked.

Auntie Gillie looked at Granny Shiela, then she said, "Mother, did Miss Daisie give you an invitation."

Pursing her lips, Granny shook her head to indicate this had not been done.

"Then we were wedding crashers too?" I asked. No one responded. Granny Shiela promised never to speak to Miss Daisie again.

Of course, the vexation only lasted for two weeks. I knew it would. When Miss Daisie turned up bearing a piece of the wedding cake, Granny Shiela gave the wedding gift to Miss Daisie. "For de young people," she said gruffly.

Uncle Tom promised never to accept an invitation from Miss Daisie again! Such an embarrassment—to be associated with wedding crashers!

Guided Questions

1. What are the names of the characters planning to get married?

2. Where is the wedding ceremony supposed to take place?

3. What phrase did Miss Daisie use to suggest it was time the young people got married?

4. "He herded them" is associated with which figure of speech?

5. Why was Miss Daisie involved in the wedding?

6. Explain in our own words the phrase "to man the door".

7. Identify two examples of similes used in this story and say why they are used appropriately.

8. What is the difference between the "wedding watchers" and the "wedding crashers"?

9. Another figure of speech introduced in this chapter is the pun. Find an example of its use.

10. What reason does Granny Shiela use for not wanting to travel far for the wedding ceremony?

11. There are two things that distressed Uncle Tom just before the wedding. Name them.

Discussion

The word "courting" is rather old fashioned. What are some of the terms used when a young man and young woman have a romantic interest in each other and are going out together?

What new practices are now used instead of giving extravagant gifts?

What does the phrase "walking on eggshells" mean?

Additional Work

Add new figures of speech to those you have already compiled.

Practise making sentences to understand the meaning of the words consternation and rampant.

Chapter Fourteen

Queen ah Sheba!

Mrs. Agatha France lived in the swankiest side of the village with her "one girl chile". Her daughter, Francelia France, called "F squared" or "Queen ah Sheba" behind her back, did not talk to people in the village. I could have sworn that Francelia's feet never touched the ground. At ten years old I was looking for a role model, and what impressed me most about Francelia was the way she spoke. She was eighteen years old. Her hair was thick, long and curly, and she wore it loosely around her shoulders, so its movement matched her dainty steps.

Many evenings, I stood in front the mirror practising how to look down my nose, squinching up my eyes or pursing my lips the way Francelia did. Francelia France was an example of what I wanted to be when I grew older— tall and elegant, and well-shaped. Miss Daisie said her personal seamstress had told her a well-shaped woman was one whose waist was ten inches less than her chest and twelve inches less than her hips. At that time my chest, waist and hips were all the same.

At least Alicia is half-way there, I thought sourly. She had filled out, and her womanly shape was becoming more and more visible each day.

The newspaper highlighted Francelia's achievements. Not only was she good-looking, she was also intelligent. She won a scholarship to one of the most prestigious schools in town—Bishop's High School—and she represent-ed the country at a French quiz held in Guadeloupe. When Francelia came back to Golden Grove she would shrug her shoulders and flutter her hands and speak with an accent in the way the French people did, I suppose. And that was not the only award Francelia had received. She had won three beau-ty contests so far in the country—Miss Teen, Miss Valentine, and Miss May

Flower! Miss Daisie said that young men in the village really admired her, but from afar, since she spoke to no one.

Old Mr. Parson would call out, "Good morning your Ladyship", but Francelia did not spare him a glance.

Miss Daisie smiled and tried to 'suck up' asking, "How is yuh modder, Francelia?" To this question, Francelia responded with a monosyllabic, "Fine." Her lips hardly moved.

"I wonder if she has teeth in her mouth?" Alicia mused. "You ever see her smile?" She directed the question to me, knowing full well I could not answer. Alicia was quite irritated that I had a bad case of hero-worship, or was it heroine-worship, for Francelia.

"Dat girl too big for her boots," Granny Shiela grumbled. "One day she gwine get her comeuppance." She nodded emphatically as if it were a done deal.

"She passes people straight in the road," Aunty Gillie complained. "Not even a good morning or good afternoon. Is like Mrs. France never teach her good manners."

"Well, people say manners maketh man and not woman," Uncle Tom interjected. I knew he was poking fun at Auntie Gillie because he was trying to hide a smile.

Miss Daisie, being another 'put-it-to-right' like Miss Maxwell the village matriarch, went to Mrs. Agatha France with some friendly advice. She mentioned Francelia was at the right age for young men to start courting her, and Francelia needed to be more outgoing and friendly. Miss Daisie even mentioned that some of the young men called Francelia "sour puss" because of her unfriendly disposition.

Mrs. France was not amused. She told Miss Daisie in no uncertain terms that she, Miss Daisie, was the worst person to talk about anybody "chile". Mrs. France reminded Miss Daisie it was because she (Miss Daisie) smiled so much with all those men she did not have a "chick or a chile", and her name had been called for mashing up so many marriages. When Miss Daisie relayed the outcome of her visit to Granny Shiela, there were tears in her eyes.

"Ah didn't mean bad, Shiela," Miss Daisie's said, her voice thick.

"Yuh don't worry Daisie," Granny Shiela was angry on her friend's behalf. "Miss France should be de last person to talk. Remember we did ketch she in de back seat..." Her voice trailed away when she realized that I was like the nosy, pesky lizard, ready to absorb what they were saying.

"Yuh hear how de mother of dis girl you admire so much, does treat people?" Granny Shiela was bristling with anger.

I tried to defend my idol. "Granny Shiela, you can't blame Francelia for the way her mother behaves."

"What yuh know chile?" Granny Shiela argued. "Children are a product of deir home environment. Dat girl behaving just how she modder used to behave. And one day, you mark my words, she will pay for her stuck-up ways." There was finality in Granny Shiela's words.

I stayed silent. I had the highest respect for Granny Shiela's prophesies. Aunty Gillie said Granny Shiela had 'goat mouth' and her words could blight people.

Two nights later, I was quite sure the gods were fighting in the sky, and the end of the world was near. Lightning flashed, thunder boomed, and the heaven opened its window and drenched the earth. I endured the racket for a while before I bolted for Granny Shiela's room.

"Yuh getting too big fuh dis," Granny Shiela, grumbled as she shifted her bulk on the bed to make room for me. I snuggled down in the warm space that Granny Shiela had occupied, then closed my eyes.

"De country really need a wash out," Granny Shiela's voice rumbled, "but most importantly plenty people will learn to fear God. Every time we have such bad rains, people does remember to tink of deir wicked deeds."

I awoke the next morning to a hunch in my side. "Yuh ain't getting up?" Granny Shiela's voice was irritable. "Ah got a pain in my left foot cause you almost push me outta me own bed. Rain finish fall. Go back to de room you and Alicia sharing."

I stretched lazily before I scooted out the bed and padded to my room. Alicia was just stirring. She wrinkled her nose at the sight of me with my blanket trailing in my wake.

"You can't grow up?" Alicia groaned. "Go use the bath first. I want a little more sleep."

I stumbled back out the room, leaving the blanket in a heap on the floor.

"You heard the thunder last night?" Auntie Gillie asked excitedly. "I swear say a lightning bolt fall somewhere in town."

"How she could hear when she was sprawled out on my bed?" Granny Shiela shuffled into the room.

"Sue!" Auntie Gillie wailed reproachfully. "Not again!"

I kept silent as I went into the shower shivering as the cold water pummeled my body.

I desperately hoped the school yard would be flooded and the roof would leak so badly the classrooms would be uninhabitable. Then we would get the day off or days for that matter! No one should go to school when it was so rainy! My wishes came through, but not in the ways I expected. First of all, the family could not leave the yard. The broad plank that connected the compound to the elevated road was below water; so no one could tell which was road or river.

"Whole night ah hear big stones tumbling in de river," Granny Shiela said. "Water reach right up to de tird step. The whole yard flooded. We don't own a canoe so yuh cyant go to school."

I screwed up my face and gave the impression I was sorry I couldn't get to school, but deep down inside I was elated. Auntie Gillie bustled around the kitchen providing a delicious lunch and a nutty banana bread for dessert. I felt pleasantly plump at the end of the day and wished for more rain to pour that night.

Unfortunately, the next morning the sun pushed through the grey clouds, and everyone went outside to see whether the broad plank had been washed away. Although the water was still high in some places, Uncle Tom said he would venture out to test the muddy ground. He hastily returned with his hind parts encased in mud. He had slipped and fallen, much to Granny Shiela's delight and Auntie Gillie's irritation. We were sent to our room to give him some privacy while he removed his trousers on the kitchen steps.

"As if we don't see men in their underwear in the magazines," Alicia pursed her lips like a sour lemon.

"It's a lucky thing he didn't break his foot," I said while Alicia rolled her eyes and mumbled "Goody two-shoes" under her breath.

A while later a loud noise came from the kitchen.

"I'm sure that is Miss Daisie's voice I am hearing," Alicia said. "I hope Uncle Tom got a chance to put on his pants." She chortled. "Can you imagine Uncle Tom's spindly legs exposed?" She burst out into loud infectious laughter. I joined in rather helplessly at the image of Miss Daisie staring at Uncle Tom's bare legs.

"Alicia, you too wicked," I said, trying to control my mirth. "It has to be something really big for Miss Daisie to brave the sludge and mud to come visiting. I am going down to find out."

"Bring back a slice of banana bread and the comess when you find out," Alicia ordered.

I quickly ran down the steps and saw Miss Daisie munching on a thick wedge of banana bread with a chilled glass of mauby. Her mouth was going like a speeding train.

"Shucks," I muttered quietly to myself. "She must have smelt the baking from quite over the road. I hope Auntie Gillie left back some for us."

"I tell yuh she haffa tank de good Lord she didn't drown. I'm sure she swallow plenty muddy river water. Is two times she went under, you know."

"What happen Miss Daisie?" I asked, while Granny Shiela gave me the 'evil eye' for interrupting. Miss Daisie emptied her glass and tinkled the ice cubes to signal she needed a refill. Auntie Gillie stared crossly at me before taking the jug of mauby to refill Miss Daisie's glass. Miss Daisie took a big gulp of the mauby.

"She has to rewind," Uncle Tom said humorously.

"I have to start from top," Miss Daisie agreed, "or you wouldn't hear everyting. It's de one Francelia France. She nearly get she dead today." Miss Daisie shook her head in satisfaction, while my mouth opened wide with shock.

"Wha...what? How you mean Miss Daisie. Someone tried to kill her?"

"Wait nah. Alyuh children too impatient," Miss Daisie looked disgruntled. "I am telling yuh de story. De one Francelia France was going to work dis morning in all dat rain—dressed to the ninety-nine wid stocking and high heel shoes, if you please. Mind you, everybody get on dey wedder boots or gym boots except she. So, when she crossed de plank to come up from her yard to de road, she slip and fall right into de river. You know when rain fall, de river does come down wid a vengeance, so de force of de water double she up. She go down one time and come up coughing. And hear dis, she try to call fuh help wid all she dixing English voice. 'Can someone please help me?'" Miss Daisie tried to mimic Francelia's refined voice. "But I hear say when she go down de second time and come up, she bawl like a cow. And hear dis, not a soul want to go and help she. Is hip shorted ole man De Souza who had to slide down de bank on he backside."

With this pronouncement, Miss Daisie stopped and looked up guiltily at Granny Shiela and the others, but everyone was too engrossed in the conversation to admonish her, so she gave a little cough and continued. "By de time he huff and puff and haul she out, Francelia France looked like dem hens dat get wet in de rain and all dey fedders stick down. She was bawling for all she wort' and must be tell ole De Souza tank yuh a million times."

"You mean she was looking bedraggled?" Uncle Tom asked, looking out the corners of his eyes at me. I nodded and filed the word away for future reference

There was silence for a while before Granny Shiela dusted her hands as though she had just finished kneading bread with flour. "Well ah hope she learn she lesson." Granny Shiela said. "You know is every year people does drown in de river and get mash up on de river stones. God gave she a second chance. We will have to wait and see."

Head bent in deep thought, I left the room and went back up to the bedroom, forgetting Alicia's request.

"Where's my slice of banana bread?" Alicia asked peevishly.

"Not now Alicia," I responded with irritation Alicia looked at me in surprise then bolted from the room to find out what had occurred. I lay on her unmade bed and reflected: *Beauty does not make you smart. Beauty does not give you the right to treat other people like dung. Yes, I admired Francelia France! Yes, I had wished on numerous occasions I could grow up just as beautiful, but I wouldn't want to change all the accolades people gave to me through Granny Shiela and Auntie Gillie, of course.*

"Sue growing up to be a mannerly young woman."

"Sue behaves very kind, caring and courteous."

"I wish my daughter would behave more like Sue. She will go very far."

And I certainly didn't want people to feel glad when something bad happened to me.

Some days later, Miss Daisie waltzed into our kitchen

"I come to bring alyuh de latest," she announced. "Is breaking news all over de village."

I stopped doing my homework while Granny Shiela sat straighter in her reclining chair. Uncle Tom pursed his lips while Auntie Gillie rolled her eyes. Alicia, as usual was in her room.

"Dis morning, de one Miss Francelia France walked down de road and say good morning to everybody she pass. Ah hear say de fellas an dem was so shocked dey couldn't even answer, and de girls and dem look round to see who she talking to." Miss Daisie looked as pleased as punch.

"Well ah hope her modder's influence was washed off in de river," Granny Shiela said. "Maybe, just maybe, dere is hope for her."

Guided Questions

1. Who is the main character in this story?
2. What is the name of the other "put it to right"?
3. What caused the conflict between Miss Daisie and Ms. France?
4. Identify any two similes and metaphors used in this chapter and explain their effectiveness.
5. The narrator makes mention of Noah and the ark in the Bible. What figure of speech is associated with such references?
6. Why did Uncle Tom look out the corners of his eyes at Sue when he used the word "bedraggled"?
7. How does Miss Daisie explain what the word "bedraggled" means?
8. Find another word for "chortled".
9. What valuable lesson does the narrator learn through this story?

Discussion

How do you react during a thunderstorm, or when you hear the news of an impending hurricane?

The narrator makes mention of a number of dishes prepared by Auntie Gillie because of the rain storm and since there was no school. Why did she do this? What is normally cooked at your house when you have an unexpected holiday because of a hurricane?

Have you ever heard the phrase "Goody two-shoes"? What does it mean? Why does Alicia call Sue by that name?

Activity

Granny Shiela says, "Children are a product of their home environment." Briefly debate the topic, "Parents are to be blamed for the way children behave at school."

Additional Work

Add new words to your word bank and figures of speech to your literacy chart.

Find out the meaning of the words used in italics and make sentences with them.

Chapter Fifteen

Village Ram

At 11 years old, there was another momentous change in my life. I sat the end of Primary School country assessment examination, known then as Common Entrance. I wasn't worried because the examination had been easy. Auntie Gillie began to fuss!

"I just hope with all the big words she does use that she pass this test high. It will determine the outcome of her life," she fretted to Uncle Tom while I sat listening to them and feeling rather irritated. Didn't they keep telling me I was bright?

"Why you harassing yourself?" Uncle Tom asked. "The girl is a natural. Is not you say that bright like a star? Just this Sunday, the Reverend called her to read the scriptures in front of the whole congregation."

"I doan know why she keep harassing de girl," Granny Shiela called out. "Sumitra Gallenger name will be in de newspapers. Watch and see!"

Sure enough, I did well when the result came out. I had passed for the prestigious Bishop's High School in the capital city of Georgetown, barely missing being the overall top performer. I started school, well decked out in my green uniform, black striped tie, knee-length white socks, and black sneakers. Auntie Gillie had laboriously covered each textbook with thick, brown paper to keep them from getting dirty.

"Yuh could sell dem when you get to form two and make a likkle small change," Granny Shiela said.

The first day of Secondary school was a nightmare! Granny Shiela insisted on accompanying Uncle Tom and Auntie Gillie to the school. Granny Shiela insisted that the security guard say if she had any training to protect all the girls from "dem tief man and bad boys" who preyed on the young girls. Granny Shiela then insisted that she meet with the principal, pulling along Uncle Tom and Auntie Gillie like a tugboat. I slinked along in their wake, silently seething. I felt mortified as students and parents stared at me. When Granny Shiela met the harassed principal, Mrs. Porter, the bewildered woman had to give her whole genealogy before Granny Shiela was satisfied that she was fit for the job as principal of the school.

"I did know yuh modder," Granny Shiela said happily, "She used to sell bread and cakes in Swanky's bakery."

"Yes, yes," Mrs. Porter said. I could see the embarrassment on her face. "Nice to meet you. So much to do." She hustled away leaving Uncle Tom pursing his lips in disapproval at Granny Shiela, and Auntie Gillie tsk-ing in embarrassment.

After that episode, I had to establish myself quickly. The teachers regarded me with suspicion (they must have heard how Granny Shiela behaved). The other girls sneered at the way I tried to speak properly, and the boys gave exaggerated bows when I passed by them before bursting into laughter. I had to force myself to go to school some days. I couldn't discuss it with my family. Granny Shiela was to be blamed in the first place! Alicia would be sure to laugh at me. She didn't get to go to the top school! As a matter of fact, she constantly harped on whether I had my bath before I came to bed, but I dismissed it as jealousy.

Instead, I applied myself diligently to my work and outperformed the entire class. My crowning glory was when I became class monitor, and the teachers acknowledged my brilliance by calling upon me to answer questions relating to new vocabulary when our classes had a House competition. Soon the other girls flocked around me and wanted to be my friend while the boys gave a nod of respect whenever I passed by.

"That child Sumitra Gallenger has a dictionary in her brain," I overheard one teacher telling another.

It was during the second term that I realized quite a few of my newly made friends were keeping away from me. My face broke out with acne and there were some spots on my legs. No one wanted to do group work with me, and I distinctly heard someone say, "Baa... ra... ram" when I was walked by.

It got so irritating I complained to my teacher who investigated the matter. When Mrs. Gopaul spoke to Mischa who was my rival for popularity in the class, she said she had just seen an old man walking by and his nickname was "Ram". Mrs. Gopaul dismissed the complaint because she said there really was an old man named Ram. The name calling continued especially whenever I passed a group of students, since it was difficult to identify the culprit.

It bothered me so much that I became quiet and withdrawn at home. It was my refusal to have dinner with the family one evening that made Auntie Gillie concerned.

"What's the matter, Sue?" she coaxed. "Tell Auntie what is bothering you."

At first, I hesitated then I asked, "Auntie Gillie, you know an old man named Ram Goat in the village?"

"Yes," Auntie Gillie replied wrinkling her nose slightly. "He lives on the seediest side of the village."

I asked her why the old man had been given such an awful nickname.

Embarrassment stained Auntie Gillie's face, before she replied. "Well, I know him since I was small, and that's what we used to call him. Let's go and ask your grandmother. She is sure to know."

Granny Shiela did know. Sitting in her favourite rocking chair, Granny Shiela sounded rather nostalgic as she said, "His real name is Sylvester Carver. He was real shy and quiet; however, people take it to mean he tought he was better dan everyone else. They get vexed dat someone who came from such poor beginnings could dare behave dat way. Den he hit puberty and everyting fall apart."

"What do you mean by puberty?" I asked curiously.

"Well, he start to turn a young man, nah," Granny Shiela said as though the information was known to one and all. "His voice start to break. He start to get hair on his chest and his chin, among odder tings." Granny Shiela paused for a while before she continued, her voice was lower. "People didn't mind dat, you know because all boys have to go trough dat stage—but was de smell."

"Smell?" my voice was puzzled.

"Yes," Granny Shiela said, "Yuh never know ram goat does smell bad. Yuh ain't remember de big ram goat Billings had and how it used to smell up de place? Because Sylvester was going tru puberty and smell so bad, people start calling him Ram Goat. And dat name stick on to him for de rest a his life."

Auntie Gillie had continued Mr. Carver's life story, relating that he couldn't get a girlfriend because his perspiration smelt so high. The girls were too ashamed to go out with someone whose nickname was Ram Goat. "He had a nervous breakdown as well, for he had really loved a young woman. She married his best friend." she concluded

I felt really sorry for Mr. Carver.

The conversation did not stop there. Auntie Gillie shared, "Both girls and boys go through puberty. They may break out in acne spots on their faces or their perspiration smells really high." Auntie Gillie's voice trailed away. She and Granny Shiela looked at each other wide-eyed.

Tears welled up in my eyes. "The girls were calling ME Ram Goat."

"Come here," Granny Shiela ordered. As soon as I got near, she grabbed me and began sniffing like a dog searching for a bone. "Jesus. Yuh smell bad fuh true. Yuh bade since you come home?"

"Not yet, Granny," I mumbled. "It's only six o'clock."

"Go and bade right now," Granny Shiela ordered. As I rushed out the sitting room, I heard Granny Shiela say, "Gillie, you shudda be more observant. De girl want turn young lady right under we nose."

The next day, Auntie Gillie collected me after school, and we went to town. There Auntie Gillie bought a sweet smelling Bath and Body Works cream and two expensive bottles of perfume. "One is for school, and one for home," Auntie Gillie said. "Tonight, we are going out for ice-cream, just the two of us. We have to talk about changes in young women."

I felt a bit ashamed. For all the knowledge I was bent on acquiring, I never thought of a girl's life-changing cycle. In a subdued voice, I asked Auntie Gillie, "Why didn't Mr. Carver's family get him some deodorant? It would have saved him so much pain and embarrassment."

"In those days, deodorant was a luxury. Do you know some people used to lather bath soap under their armpits?" Auntie Gillie said. "And do you know in some cultures, men who have a high perspiration are admired by women?"

"What? What?" I spluttered. "That's gross! Who would want to do that?"

"Go and research it," Auntie Gillie gave her usual advice.

Soon after that episode, I did have a change in life. According to Granny Shiela I "had come young lady". My body odour regulated, my pimples and acne faded, and I regained my popularity. It was a valuable lessons for me!. I had become so caught up with excelling in my studies that I did not pay attention to the little things like "body care" and "personal hygiene."

Guided Questions

1. Identify one clue that justifies Uncle Tom's confidence in Sue's success at the major examination.

2. Why does Auntie Gillie cover the textbooks.

3. What does the repetition of the phrase "Granny Shiela insisted" tells us about Granny Shiela's character?

4. "I slinked along, silently seething." Identify the figure of speech used in this statement.

5. State another figure of speech (apart from the one used above) used in this chapter and give an example of it. Explain why it is effective.

6. How did the principal feel about Granny Shiela's statement about her family? How do you know?

7. How does Sue establish herself as a leader in the classroom?

8. What was the real reason for the unspoken conflict between Sue and the other girls in the class? Justify your answer.

9. What are the different signs of puberty in girls as compared to boys? What is similar?

10. What lesson does the narrator learn from her experience in this story?

Discussion

Talk about similar or different practices of your parents as opposed to Sue's family. How did it make you feel?

Did your parents prepare you for puberty? Why/why not?

Chapter Sixteen

The Tailor Man

I was upset and wanted the entire village to know. I walked with my face as sour as green tamarind and just hoped I wouldn't meet anyone with whom she was good friends. How could Granny Shiela send me, a first form student of the most prestigious school, to the tailor shop in the seamiest side of the village?

"It is totally unreasonable!" I grumbled to myself as I walked in the blistering sun. Why Granny Shiela couldn't send me to the seamstresses right in the heart of Golden Grove to darn the large hole in the dress that a nail had ripped when she visited Miss May, her friend who lost a leg because of diabetes? There was Miss Badenock, then Miss Augustus and Mrs. Franklyn. Those women sewed bridal outfits, and their dresses always seemed "ready-made".

Under my breath, I imitated Granny Shiela. "Dem woman want to get rich too fast. Imagine just to hem a dress is fifteen dollar. And don't talk about if dey had to let out de seams in a dress— tirty dollar." To my mind, Granny Shiela was just too stingy! Imagine she was putting me through this strenuous journey just because Mr. Charles charged five dollars for any job. "Ridiculous!" I muttered under my breath. I almost staggered into Mr. Charles' tailor shop, glad to get out of the punishing rays of the sun. I tried to adjust my eyes from the glare of the sun and saw three shadowy figures crammed inside.

"Sun hot, eh little girl?" Mr. Charles wrinkled his nose. "It make you sweat plenty eh?" He wrinkled his nose again while the other people who were waiting there looked at Sue from the corners of their eyes. They too began to wrinkle their noses.

"*Shucks!*" my mind screamed. "*I forget to put on deodorant.*"

"Granny Shiela send me," I blurted out. "She wants you to hem..."

"Yu have to wait yuh turn," interrupted an old woman. "I here waiting very long. And dat young boy reach here before yuh."

I stayed dumb, my head bent. I was not going to entertain these people in any discussion. I could not understand why some adults could be so rude! The "bad words" that sneaked into my mind whenever I got angry usually gave me an instant headache. My mind seemed to relish repeating the obscenities and at some inconvenient times in school, such words were known to fly out of my mouth involuntarily. It was only the grace of God that prevented Auntie Gillie or the principal from hearing of it! The old woman soon had her turn, mended her satin church dress and left.

"What you want me to do for you, young man?" asked Mr. Charles.

I didn't even realise a boy from my school was in the shop! Darting a suspicious glance at me, he mumbled softly.

"You want to take in de pants foot?" Mr. Charles exposed the boy's business. "How you going walk? Alyuh young people and dese styles."

The boy mumbled again, then Mr. Charles retorted, "I'm going to take one inch on each pant legs right up to de crotch. Yuh will try it on first before I take it in furdder."

The machine whirred loudly and in a short while Mr. Charles handed the boy the pants.

"Go behind de counter and try it on." He suggested. There was not much room to manoeuvre as the place was cluttered with an old machine and bundles of bags containing scrap material. If the boy were to take off his pants, I was sure to get an eyeful. The boy looked at me suspiciously once again. We had a staring match before I conceded, left the small shop and allowed him his privacy. I returned just in time to hear their parting conversation.

"See what I say," Mr. Charles crowed when the boy came around to show how the pants fit him. He held out his hand, collected the payment and turned round to face me.

"Now young lady, what Miss Shiela say?"

"Granny asked if..." Before I could continue, a young woman barrelled into the shop as though propelled by an unseen hand.

"Mr. Charles, the girl could wait. I have an emergency."

"Everybody does be in a hurry on Friday mornings," Mr. Charles said irritably.

The young lady was flawlessly made up. Her face smooth and brown, full lips artfully outlined in deep purple and her hair in burgundy spikes.

"Mr. Charles, you can't remember me?" the young lady's voice had changed from being commanding to coaxing. "My mother name is Theresa. She used to live four doors away from you before she went to the U.S."

Mr. Charles conveniently forgot that I had been waiting a while.

"Yesss," he said, "I did miss her fuh true. Is 'Merica she went? So what happen to yuh grandmodder?"

The conversation became animated as these two unlikely acquaintances reminisced about people who lived here and there and what their lives had become. I began tapping my feet. My irritation knew no bounds. *Adults could be so inconsiderate*, I thought. *Like midnight going to find me in Mr. Charles's tailor shop.*

The young woman changed the topic so smoothly, it took a full minute for Mr. Charles to understand what she was saying and for me to stop venting in my mind.

"So Mr. Charles, I buy this pair of white pants in the States, and it was fitting me well you know, but now I put the pants on today, the crotch hang down. It's not fitting me close. I want you to take in the sides by the crotch so it can fit me properly. Right now it fitting me like if I am a man, you know."

Mr. Charles eyes bulged in horror as the young woman unceremoniously unbuttoned her white jeans and started to drag it down.

"Stop!" Mr. Charles wheezed out. I thought he was going to faint. "Go behind the counter."

"Eh, eh," the young lady remarked. "Mr. Charles you never see a naked woman. My mother say you did have a foreign woman, but your mother run her out of Golden Grove." My eyes were like ping-pong balls as I stared at the young woman, then at Mr. Charles to see what they both would do.

"Give me de pants, let me see what I can do," Mr. Charles ignored the young woman's words and held out his hand. She picked up an unused piece of cloth from the counter and wrapped it around her lower body, then handed the pants to Mr. Charles. Her lips were pursed in irritation. In the meantime, I waited for Mr. Charles to respond to her statement about his earlier life. The whirring of the machine was all the response that came from him,

After Mr. Charles had adjusted the pants' crotch twice, the young woman claimed she was satisfied and collected the pants, donned them on, handed Mr. Charles a twenty-dollar bill and sailed out of the shop.

Mr. Charles turned to me. "Now young lady what you say Ms. Shiela want me to do wid dis dress?" His forehead was furrowed and his voice laced with irritation. Grabbing the dress out of my hand and without giving me a chance to respond, he said, "What she know 'bout me? She modder had to run outta Golden Grove and go 'Merica because she and Miss Daisie had one helluva fight over Mrs. Latchmie husband. It was de worst scandal I tell you. Me? I can't dey wid black women. De lady was from Germany. You know where dat is?" Once again I did not get a chance to answer.

"She was very educated and didn't mind walking all over de place wid me. If yuh know how many fellas try to take she way? But she didn't bodder wid dem. She went back cause she is a journalist, yuh know? I couldn't go wid her cause I haffa look after me modder. She old and cyant do fuh she self. You understand?" Of course, I didn't quite understand, but I listened in shock and amazement as Mr. Charles gave me the history of his relationship with the German woman named Gretchen.

By the time Mr. Charles handed me Granny Shiela's dress, my mind was teeming with questions. Moreso, when Mr. Charles refused payment, stating that he and Granny Shiela "did sweet on each odder" in the early days and Granny Shiela had gotten pregnant for a Cassanova who liked to "play de girls".

My granny was involved in such a scandal? I thought in disbelief as I left Mr. Charles' shop.

When I got home, Granny Shiela was waiting impatiently. "Where you been so long?" she asked crossly.

"Granny Shiela, plenty people were in the shop and when it was my turn, a young lady came in, start to pull down her pants." I was eager to share all the gossip I had heard.

"Dat old lecher still up to his tricks?" Granny's voice quivered with outrage. "Dat is why I had to leave him in de first place." My mouth fell open, and Granny Shiela came to an abrupt stop.

"So Granny, is true you and Mr. Charles was boyfriend and girlfriend?" I asked in astonishment. "The German lady take him away from you?" But Granny kept tight-lipped, grabbed her dress, and went into her room mumbling to herself.

My relationship with Alicia had its bright moments, especially when I wanted to find out some gossip related to the village. She seemed to know people's business, and I never asked her how she knew. Alicia explained that Mr. Charles was a gentleman in his days. People regarded him as a gentleman because he was an attentive son. He was the only child for his mother. He accompanied her to the market, holding her basket as she shopped, and he even helped other older women with their shopping bags as well. When he and Granny Shiela started seeing each other, Mr. Charles' mother asked him to take her home to make an introduction. After Mrs. Charles saw Granny Shiela she found many imperfections—her face was too broad, so too were her nose and mouth. And worst of all she was too black.

"So why he didn't marry the German woman?" I whispered.

"Mr. Charles' mother say Gretchen wanted to rule her son because he did all the housework. They used to live wid her you see. One day Mrs. Charles beat Gretchen wid an umbrella and chased her out the house. That was the end of the relationship. Now he just exists on memories." Alicia's voice faded as she prepared to sleep.

Three months later, Granny Shiela sent me to Mr. Charles once again. I wasn't happy, but I went anyway. This time Mr. Charles sat alone sewing what looked like a piece of rag.

"How are you, Mr. Charles," I chirped, "and how is your friend Gretchen from Germany?"

Mr. Charles looked owlishly over his rimless spectacles, his face in an irritated grimace, "Her name is Hilda and she from Sweden," he responded.

"Sorry," I replied, rolling my eyes like Alicia usually did because I was sure he had said Germany, "Granny Shiela send this blouse. It has a rip in the shoulder."

I had already figured out Mr. Charles. He really had no woman friend—he was past the age for girlfriend—and lived out his own fantasies of the "could have, should have been".

"Yuh know who win de football match between Guyana and El Salvador?" Mr. Charles asked as he snipped and cut the material.

"No, Mr. Charles," I responded.

"Must be El Salvador win", he mumbled. Suddenly he looked up and said, "Is not dat we country cyant play good you know, but we frighten de name of de people. You know what I mean?"

"Yes, Mr. Charles," I said meekly.

"Is just like Satan. Satan frighten we. Yuh understand what I mean?"

"Yes, Mr. Charles." I couldn't understand how God came into the conversation.

"Is only because God is a spirit. He did fight Satan yuh know. Yuh understand what I mean?"

I stood there for the next fifteen minutes, parroting, "Yes, Mr. Charles. I hear you, Mr. Charles. I agree, Mr. Charles," wishing desperately someone else would come and release me from Mr. Charles' ranting about the devil and El Salvador. At last an elderly man stopped by. Mr. Charles shoved the blouse into my hand and without missing a beat began to engage the man in conversation about El Salvador, the football team and "going to hell". I vowed to ask Granny Shiela to let Alicia bring her clothes the next time.

Guided Questions

1. (a) How does the setting contribute to theme of the story?
   (b) Which important part does it play?
   (c) What does it tell us about Mr. Charles?

2. Why was the narrator upset?

3. Why did Granny Shiela chose to send her clothes specifically to Mr. Charles?

4. Why do you think Mr. Charles "wrinkled his nose" after mentioning to the narrator the sun was hot?

5. Why did the narrator and the boy have a "staring match"?

6. Why did the young woman feel entitled to have her pair of pants adjusted before the narrator although she was there first?

7. Use one adjective to appropriately describe Mr. Charles. Explain why you selected that adjective.

8. What is the valuable lesson Sue learned after her encounter with Mr. Charles?

Discussion

Have you ever been waiting in a line and someone pushes in? Share your experience and mention how you felt at that particular time.

Tailors and seamstresses are a "dying breed". Why do you think this is so?

Chapter Seventeen

Drunk and Disorderly

The upbeat music of the Mighty Sparrow's "Drunk and Disorderly" was loud, interrupting the flood of memories and changing the direction of my thoughts. I shifted in my chair, trying to find a comfortable position. Uncle Tom often played this song on our antiquated gramophone. It made a such great impression on me that when I decided to get married I vowed never to marry a man who drank alcohol just like Mr. Murphy.

Jeffrey Murphy lived two houses away from us, but since most of his bad behaviour occurred in the nights and sounds travelled clearly, we could hear everything that went on. The other neighbours did not get involved. Not my Granny Shiela!

I felt sorry for both his wife and children. He was short, medium-built and very respectful. Whenever he left for work he tipped his cap and called out "good morning" to Granny Shiela who sat in her usual spot on the porch. He was a port worker, helping to offload the cargo in Georgetown when the ships came in from England or America. Granny Shiela said he was the un-luckiest man she knew. Her voice lowered when she shared with Auntie Gil-lie that Mr. Murphy had planned to marry a pretty girl who had his complex-ion, but found out she was his father's "outside" daughter. I was at the table listening in while pretending to do my homework. As Alicia became older, she was sometimes allowed to listen to certain "big people" conversation.

"I doan know how he ain't end up in de mad house," Granny Shiela's voice rumbled softly. "Ah does really try to understand he. All now so, he cyant get over his first love." After the big scandal, according to Granny Shiela, "Mur-phy didn't care if Sunday fall on a Monday."

Alicia and I exchanged glances, then I asked, "So why he get married to somebody else?"

Granny Shiela shooed us like chickens, "Y'all too fast and want to get in big people business." She conveniently forgot that she shared the information without us asking anything. I grumbled under my breath, "Old people...." It did not bear contemplating what would happen if she heard me.

Mr. Murphy's marriage had produced five children; two of the children had taken his complexion, while the other three were dark-skinned like their mother—and therein was the problem!

Every Friday night, Mr. Murphy would stop off at a rum shop in the seediest side of the village. There he became talkative and got into loud arguments on topics ranging from politics to cricket and football, or a picture he had seen. Sometimes, Mr. Murphy would leave the rum shop at nine o'clock in the night, weaving from side to side and having a one-sided conversation.

"You too lie," Mr. Murphy would shout out, startling any passer-by. He never waited for an answer and continued his dialogue with himself. "How you mean I lie? I bet you a hundred dollars now, is de truth I telling you."

At other times, Mr. Murphy would get into fist fights with his drinking partners. They would break up stools and tables in the rums shops; police would be called in, and Mr. Murphy would spend the night in the lock-up. One rum shop owner became so fed up, he decided to press charges against Mr. Murphy, who was fined by the magistrate for behaving "drunk and disorderly".

"It's like he enjoys spending a night in de village police station," Granny Shiela said crossly.

Every Friday night (if he wasn't locked up at the village station) I listened for Mr. Murphy's approach. When he got to about a hundred yards from his home, the volume of his voice would increase. He started with hymns, "Nearer My God to Thee!" or he would make up his own composition, the words making absolutely no sense. I found this rather hilarious as I listened to his off-key voice ringing out in the still, evening air. I just knew that his children would end up over at our house. I nudged Alicia awake.

"It's no use pretending to sleep. Murphy is drunk again and Granny Shiela will just come to wake us up."

We wandered into the sitting room.

"Murphy in his cups again," Uncle Tom muttered in resignation.

"Gillie, use de blanket to make up some beds in Alicia dem room," Granny Shiela's voice was resigned. "Dat man have demons riding him."

"You can say that again," Uncle Tom responded. "Just last month when he finally sobered up at the police station and they allowed him to leave, he meet Mr. Craigg going down the road 'bout two o'clock with his milk pan. Remember, Mr. Craigg got to walk to the pasture on the other side of Sion Hill to milk his cows. Like some of the rum was till in Murphy head cause he walk up to Mr. Craigg, chucked him off then lift he up. He throw Craigg and he milk pan across the road."

"What?" Alicia and I cried out in horror. "He's so strong to do that?" Alicia queried.

"Rum does make man turn demon," Granny Shiela repeated.

"Mr. Craigg and his milk pan went clanging down the road," Uncle Tom said, shaking his head. "Mr. Craigg didn't live too long after that. I am sure it was the hard lash he got when he fell."

"Nobody didn't report him to the police?" Alicia asked. "He should have been held accountable."

"If he goes to jail, who will mind de children?" Granny Shiela asked.

"You," I mumbled under my breath.

By this time, Mr. Murphy had passed our house and was going full steam with "When the Roll is Called up Yonder".

"Wait for it," Auntie Gillie said. And sure enough there was a loud crash.

"Bring out de children," Mr. Murphy thundered.

It was a usual occurrence if he made it home on Friday nights. Mr. Murphy would line up the children against the wall and count them again and again telling his wife he was sure they had six children. Somewhere in the recesses of his mind, he had not come to terms with the miscarriage his wife had experienced.

Sleepy or not, the children had to stand still and give their names to their father. When he got to the three dark ones, he would stop counting and then the expletives would begin. "Dese are not my children! Christabel what yuh do wid my children?" and he would begin sharing licks, not to the children but their mother. No matter how Miss Christabel cried and pleaded, Mr. Murphy would continue he licks until she ran and locked herself in the bedroom. Following this, there would be the sound of wares crashing to the floor and the splintering of wood before he collapsed amidst the ruins of his kitchen and felt into a deep sleep, emitting loud snores.

Soon after, Miss Christabel would come over, crying her heart out. The three darker children trailed behind, two of them with thumbs in their mouths and looking rather bewildered. They had been awakened from their beds once again.

By the time Miss Christabel had arrived, Auntie Gillie had three cups of warm chocolate tea, and the children gladly drank the tea before they tottered off to sleep until the next morning.

"God bless you, Miss Shiela," Miss Christabel choked out. "Murphy is a good man, you know. I don't know why he does drink so much."

Granny Shiela waited until Miss Christabel had left before she said, "An unhappy, disappointed man is a cross to bear in any relationship. I wudda left he tail from de time he start wid dat foolishness."

"Mother, the woman loves her husband," Auntie Gillie protested.

"What's love got to do wid it?" Granny Shiela retorted.

Early Saturday morning, Mr. Murphy came over as he usually did. By that time the three children had awakened and had been given breakfast by Auntie Gillie.

"Miss Shiela," Mr. Murphy said, his face red with embarrassment. "I don't know what get into me last night. I am very sorry. I love all my children." He looked at the three children, held out his arms and hugged them closely when they ran to him. He lifted the youngest into his arms and the other two held on to his pants as he led them home.

The pattern continued unabated for two years. At the village concert, one of the participants even sang about Mr. Murphy, naming the song "From

Orderly to Disorderly." But just when Granny Shiela was ready to stop being the "Good Samaritan", Mr. Murphy got ill. The doctor said he had cirrhosis of the liver, and if Mr. Murphy didn't stop drinking he would die sooner rather than later.

Luckily, Mr. Murphy followed the doctor's advice. No more disorderly noises were heard, Miss Christabel became a happy and contented woman, and the children slowly lost the frightened look in their eyes when they saw their father. Auntie Gillie and Uncle Tom put Alicia and me to sit down. With wagging fingers and shaking heads, they warned us never to marry a man who drank like a fish or smoked like a chimney.

Guided Questions

1. What caused the conflict between Mr. Murphy and his wife? Find the evidence to support your answer.

2. Write down a word that means the same as "drunk".

3. Why do you think Mr. Murphy had easy access to alcohol?

4. Do you think Mr. Murphy should have been jailed? Explain.

5. What role did Sue's family play in Mr. Murphy's life?

6. Write down the sentence that reflects the use of onomatopoeia in this story.

7. What does the phrase "chucked him off" mean? Write this colloquial expression in your own words.

8. What is the name given to people who are unable to stop drinking alcohol?

9. What was the reason Mr. Murphy rejected three of his children? Which theme can you relate to this?

Discussion

Why do people drink alcohol? Do you think men drink more alcohol than women? Explain.

Do you think children should be able to choose their parents? Explain.

Additional Work

Keep adding to your word bank and literary chart.

Activity

Write a skit and role play a court scene where Mr. Murphy is put on trial for domestic abuse.

Chapter Eighteen

Embarrassed Beyond Measure!

There are three things the older generation of my time used to say, "not all skin teet' is laff", "when yuh tink is bush is people" and "when yuh too full of yuhself, yuh riding for a fall."

I breezed through second form with the highest percentage the school recorded for any individual. As a result, I was featured in the school magazine, interviewed by people from the radio station, and had my picture in the "Daily Globe". I had students swarming around me, and even the boys in form three began to notice me by giving me "sweet eye" whenever they saw me. Things changed, however, when a girl named Chloe began attending our school.

She started in the second form because she had completed first form in Zambia, the country of her birth. Her mother, who was a diplomat, had been sent to work in Guyana from Zambia. Chloe spoke with a charming accent and had a deep-throated laugh. Everyone flocked around her, including my best friends Mandy and Daniele, who soon prefaced whatever they said with, "Chloe said this, or Chloe said that...". I was not pleased or amused when they tried to use the affected accent. Not only so, but one of the boys, who Mandy said seemed to like me, appeared to like Chloe since he would walk around the school compound with her.

Things came to a head when we had our monthly test and...wonder of wonders...Chloe came first, and I came third! Third! Those girls—I thought they were my friends!—began to snigger behind my back.

When I confronted Daniele about it, she was quick to point out, "I'm laughing with you, not at you". I saw the fake smile plastered on her face.

"I'm surprised you did so poorly this term," Mrs. Gopaul said, disappointment quite evident in her voice. You'd think I had done the worst in the class! To add fire to this flame, someone's mother had called Auntie Gillie and told her. So it became a matter of reproach, quarrelling and what's not at home. For once, Alicia seemed to feel sorry for me and tried to defend me against Granny Shiela.

"Come on, Granny," Alicia protested. "You can't crucify her for coming third once in her life! That's not fair!"

Granny Shiela would not back down. "She have a point to prove," she said mulishly.

"To whom?" Uncle Tom asked.

"All dese people who does be watching everyting we do." Granny Shiela responded immediately.

I sat there feeling quite sorry for myself for a while, then I made up my mind, *This won't happen to me again!*

I started spending time in the library and studying extra hours in the evening. The first test we had after that incident, I came first and Chloe came second.

"Good job!" Mandy smiled but the congratulations sounded fake since she quickly moved away to join the crowd around Chloe to offer her sympathy. It was as if my friends were angry with me for doing well. Nevertheless, I soon found my rhythm and began doing well once again. I kept Mandy and Daniele at a distance, but they seemed to know my weakness. I was attracted to Jared and told Mandy.

Jared was a cute boy from the third form and all of us in the class had a crush on him. He was the class monitor and also a peer counsellor. I felt I had made a greater impression on him since I was the brightest in my class. I mean everybody knew me! And more importantly, he would smile at me whenever we met in the corridor.

Although we never actually spoke to each other, this did not stop me from fantasizing about him professing his love for me. One day, five of us were in the area of the school canteen when he passed by. "Good morning ladies," he said, and we chorused our responses. From the corner of my eyes, I saw Mandy fanning herself, while Daniele held her chest as though she were having palpitations.

"What's wrong with you all?" I asked.

"He is so mannerly and respectful," Daniele said. "I think I could fall in love...." Her voice trailed away when we stared at her

"What...what?" Daniele asked.

I opened my big mouth and said, "You don't qualify. He is bright. I am bright. Do the math."

That's when the quarrel began, and our friendship began to fizzle out. Daniele and Mandy ganged up with Chloe, and they stopped talking to me. I pretended I didn't care and tried to make new friends, but it was not the same. Then there was a buzz around the class. Chloe had gone up to Jared in a rather brazen manner and began to chat him up.

One of my new friends, Jolisha, said very loudly, "She needs to go back to where she came from."

"I agree," I said nodding my head just as Mandy passed by. The animosity among us became more visible.

It was a Friday morning when another one of my newly made friends, Krista, came up to me and whispered, "Jared wants you to write him a letter if you are really interested in him."

"I don't believe you," I blurted out.

"Why would I lie?" she opened her eyes widely. "I know his younger sister and can give it to her to give to him," she offered.

Just then Jared passed by, smiled and nodded and went on his way. I took that as a sign that he was really interested in me.

That weekend I laboured over the letter I planned to send to Jared. I must have torn up ten sheets of paper before I was satisfied. In it I shared why I felt we would be a good match.

"What are you so taken up doing in your room?" Auntie Gillie asked.

"An assignment," I responded, but I hid what I had written.

I sneaked into the study and "borrowed" one of Uncle Tom's envelopes, folded the letter, sealed it in the envelope, and wrote Mr. Jared Moore neatly on it.

On Monday morning, I gave Krista the letter and sat back waiting for a response.

At recess time, I saw the boys in the class looking at me with pity, while the girls were sniggering behind their hands. I had a bad premonition, so I went looking for Krista. I found her in a huddle with Mandy, Daniele, and Chloe. She hurried towards me.

"Oh Sue," she said with a smile that did not reach her eyes. "I forgot to give you the response Jared sent."

She went into her pencil case, pulled out a letter and thrust it into my hands. I turned and walked away, my hands were sweaty, and my heart was beating fast. I was suspicious, yet there was a small spark of hope within me. When I got to the bathroom, I entered one of the stalls and closed the door. Trembling, I stared at the envelope. I tore it open quickly. There was one sheet of paper. On it there was a sentence of seven words, "Whoever told you that I like you?"

I felt my stomach heave, and I began retching. My face was hot with shame and embarrassment. The tears rained down my face. I didn't know what to do with the paper. I must have stayed in that bathroom stall for half an hour. Little did I know that a small group of girls was outside the bathroom waiting for me to emerge. When the bell rang for class to restart after recess they had to leave.

I made my way to the principal's office and asked permission to go home.

"What's wrong Sue?" Mrs. Porter asked quietly. I broke down and told her everything. She listened attentively, then picked up the telephone and called Auntie Gillie to come to collect me from school. Next, she went to my class and collected my book bag.

The principal looked at me and said, "There is nothing wrong in having your first crush, Sue. As a matter of fact, you may feel this way many times, but it is not the end of the world. It puzzles me however, that Jared Moore could be so cruel." She shook her head. "I will investigate this matter."

Auntie Gillie saw my tear-stained face and didn't ask a question. She just hugged me tightly and took me home. Granny Shiela didn't say a word either. The entire household was quiet.

That evening, Auntie Gillie asked me if I wanted to talk about what had happened at school. I hesitated before I nodded. We went into the porch. There I told Auntie Gillie all about what had transpired. Of course, I was bawling by the time I got done.

Auntie Gillie said, "You are on the threshold of becoming a teenager, Sue, so you will experience all kinds of emotions. What is important is for you to chat with me about it. Don't ever feel scared to tell me what you are feeling. Okay? It's situations like this that make young people get a nervous breakdown." Her hug became a tight squeeze before she gave me a glass of sorrel and sent me to bed.

I didn't go to school for two days. However, I heard through Auntie Gillie, what took place in my class. Mrs. Porter found out that Mandy, Daniele, and Chloe had plotted to embarrass me. They got Krista involved and read the letter I wrote before they crafted a response. Mrs. Porter called in their parents, and they all agreed the girls should be suspended for three days.

Granny Shiela was beside herself with anger. "De parents need to cut dey backside," she fumed.

Uncle Tom nodded his head and said, "Unless they change, they will grow up to be horrible young women."

Alicia waited until we got into our room and said gruffly, "It's all a part of growing up!"

When I returned to school, we had a class meeting. The four girls had to apologize to me in front of the class and Mrs. Porter spoke to us about the danger of jealousy, pride,r and spitefulness. We all learned a lesson from that incident, but I didn't regain my friendship with Mandy and Daniele. Chloe's mother was transferred to another country, so she left the school, and Jared did have a conversation with me, expressing how badly he felt about what the girls did.

In retrospect, I had been "riding for a fall" because I thought being brighter than everyone was all that mattered. It was a painful but valuable lesson. I filed away this knowledge so I would not make that mistake again.

I now had an awareness that some of the so-called friends I had were secretly jealous of me. I realised as well that the school culture needed to focus on the positive. Too many boys and girls were glad about the failure of others and talked badly about them. I desperately hoped that as we grew older, and our attitudes would change.

Guided Questions

1. What is the setting of this story?
2. Who are the major characters, apart from the narrator?
3. Identify the major themes that are explored in the story.
4. In your own words, say what you think was the real issue that caused the friendship between the girls to disintegrate.
5. Identify the mood of the narrator (i) before she wrote the letter and (ii) after she received the answer.
6. How does the narrator family show their support for her?
7. Briefly describe the relationship between Sue and Auntie Gillie.
8. What is the moral lesson of this story?

Discussion

What are some of the emotional changes associated with the teenage stage in life?

There are three colloquial expressions used at the beginning of this story. Explain what they mean.

What other colloquial expressions can you associate with this story?

Activity

Pretend that you are the class counsellor. Give a speech to your class about adolescent love.

Chapter Nineteen

The Village Crier

Miss Clarissa Green lived four houses away from us in a small wooden structure surrounded by hundreds of potted plants. She had moved into the village about a year ago and kept to herself. Derek was her canine companion, and it followed her to the market and to church. These were the two places Miss Clarissa visited as often as she could because they were within walking distance from her home. Derek was not allowed on any transport because he wanted to sit next to Miss Clarissa and would bristle and growl if anyone went near her. On a few occasions, when Derek was locked inside his pen, I would sometimes sneak over and let him out so we could romp and play. He never growled at me.

Granny Shiela would suck her teeth and warn me to desist from going onto the Miss Clarissa's yard.

"Granny Shiela, why don't you like Miss Clarissa?" I probed. "She always gives me sweets or cookies whenever I pass by. She says I am a nice girl."

"I don't dislike de woman," Granny Shiela said. "Our Christian duty is to love everybody, but my spirit just don't tek she."

"I know her from before she came to live in our village, but I can't remember when at the moment," Uncle Tom interjected.

"Strange woman," Auntie Gillie muttered, her head bent over some tangled pieces of wool.

"Quite crazy if you ask me," Alicia spoke en sotto, but Granny Shiela still heard her.

"Is not nice to call people names," Granny Shiela said sternly.

"That girl has a chip on the shoulder as big as the Rock of Gibraltar," Uncle Tom said shaking his head sadly.

Another place of interest for Miss Clarissa was the village library. I was intrigued by the different characters who visited the library. A scholarly-looking gentleman painstakingly wrote notes from the big tomes he pulled off the shelf. They were scattered all over his table. At another table an old man sat surrounded by a pile of magazines he had borrowed from the reference section.

Giggling teenage girls whispered softly, casting a furtive look at the security guard who, at intervals, would bark, "No talking in the library!" Also a number of teen-aged couples from well-known secondary schools were there gazing star-struck into each other's eyes instead of studying from the opened textbooks in front of them.

Miss Clarissa did not fit in with the normal crowd during her weekly visits, with her multi-coloured turban wrapped tightly around her head and her spectacles perched snugly on her nose. The students were terrified of her because Miss Clarissa religiously targeted the students. She would stride purposefully towards a group of students, pull up a chair, select her target and ask rather sternly, "How is your mother?"

The students, gazed wide-eyed at her before one of them, manners ingrained from the cradle, muttered, "Fine, thank you." That was the sum-total of their conversation. The students fidgeted; Miss Clarissa nodded as if they had asked a question, gave a vacant smile and stared at them. Then the tears began. "All you must behave yourself as good boys and girls. Your mother and father used to behave just so and now look at you!" Miss Clarissa sobbed bitterly. The students grabbed their books and hurried out. The security guard came rushing over and attempted to calm down Miss Clarissa before asking her to leave the library.

One of the girls who went to my church asked me, "Do you know that lady? I don't. But every time we come to the library to study, she comes up to ask about our parents and begins to cry. My parents don't know her."

"She is just an eccentric old woman," I said. "She lives on Princess street."

"Well I do not want to know her. I am very scared of her," the girl responded before hurrying away.

On Uncle Tom's 50th birthday, two major things occurred. First, a well-known individual from the steamiest side of the village died. Miss Lawson, known to everyone as Pinkie, was young and pretty, so everyone expressed shock at her early demise. Miss Daisie came over to speak with Granny Shiela, but they sent me to Mr. Hardat's grocery store. I was quite aware it was a contrived excuse to get me away from the house. Granny Shiela's excuse was there was no salt in the cupboard, but I knew a bottle filled to capacity was in that very cupboard.

When I returned home, I heard the tail end of the conversation when Miss Daisie said, "If yuh live by de sword, yuh will die by de sword. I know dat will be a very big funeral. She has family overseas so dey will have to come to help wid de funeral expenses."

The villagers were buzzing about Miss Lawson's funeral. Granny Shiela aired out her black bombazine dress, and Miss Daisie said she was wearing a purple dress since it matched her purple hat. Mr. Greaves' funeral parlour gained fame as well. He let everyone know he had ordered the casket from a South American island because they had the best mahogany caskets in the world. Granny Shiela said Alicia and I did not have to attend. We were quite glad.

On the day of the funeral, we watched the parade of colours as people came from the nearby villages to pay their respects to Miss Lawson. The younger generation wore colours that ranged from dark blue polka dots to shocking pink. They justified wearing the loud colours by saying Pinkie would not have appreciated those sombre and dreary dresses worn by the older people who turned up their noses at her and made derogatory remarks about her lifestyle.

I waited impatiently for the adults to return. I wanted the full details, or I would never be able to sleep well. When Granny Shiela, Uncle Tom and Auntie Gillie arrived, they took off their shoes at the door; Granny Shiela was adamant that shoes that walked on cemetery soil would not be allowed in the house. They collapsed tiredly in their favourite chairs.

"Well I never!" Granny Shiela began before she trailed off and stared into space.

"What happen, Granny Shiela?" I inquired eagerly, as Alicia walked into the sitting room and took up her position in the only remaining chair.

"Utter rubbish!" Uncle Tom said. Then his mouth remained open, but no further words emerged.

"So...?" Alicia gave a long-suffering sigh. "How was the funeral?"

"A fiasco!" Uncle Tom declared, dusting his hands as though he wanted no part of it.

Auntie Gillie exhaled loudly before she began. "Miss Lawson get a good send off. There were hundreds of people at the parlour. People were in the road standing. I managed to get a seat for your grandmother..."

Before Auntie Gillie could continue, Miss Daisie barged into the room without showing the least bit of courtesy.

She came straight towards me. "Girl get up. Let dis old woman rest she legs." Then she turned to face the other adults and declared with feelings, "Well, I never hear wuss!"

"What happen Miss Daisie?" I asked. I knew she would answer my question.

"Well," Miss Daisie smacked her lips, "Yuh Granny have any mauby cause I ain't start talking yet and my troat done dry?"

I hurried out and returned with a glass of cold mauby. Miss Daisie took a noisy gulp before she began.

"If yuh see a crowd ah people at dat funeral. Politicians, lawyers, doctors and even a few ah dem big shot businessmen. I say to myself, dey must be her past clients." She paused as Uncle Tom cleared his throat and Granny Shiela gave her a warning glare.

" Heh...heh," Miss Daisie gave a sheepish laugh before she continued. "Anyhow, de bacchanal start when de priest who was taking de service, ask for people to give deir tributes. 'Bout tree people come up and say what a nice person Pinkie was, and her granmodder start one bawling. Den up comes Miss Clarissa..."

"Miss Clarissa," I interjected disbelievingly. "Miss Clarissa knows Pinkie?"

"Is yuh telling de story or me?" Miss Daisie was annoyed at the interruption.

"Sorry, Miss Daisie," I said contritely. "Please carry on."

"Miss Clarissa went up an say how she did know Pinkie—from where only God knows. Den she start to say how people did envy Pinkie cause she was so bright in secondary school." Miss Daisie paused, looked at Granny Shiela and asked in disbelief, "Pinkie went secondary school?"

Granny Shiela snorted loudly, but didn't say a word.

"Next ting you know, Miss Clarissa say when Pinkie went to university de professors were jealous of her prettiness and her intelligence. One of de professors was from Haiti and he mess up she mind. Den her family did owe some rich people in town, so dey, too, mess her up." Miss Daisie paused. Granny Shiela snorted again. Auntie Gillie rolled her eyes. Alicia looked confused and I tried to process what I was hearing.

Miss Daisie continued, "By dis time, de family members from overseas start asking who was dis lady and where she come from. Pinkie never went to secondary school much less university. Nobody could understand what Miss Clarissa was talking 'bout. People start to suck dey teet and walk out of de parlour. De priest tried to get Miss Clarissa to stop de tribute, but she put down one piece ah bawling, beating she chest and stamping on de ground. While some people from outside running in to see what was de commotion, odders were running outside to get away from it. It was a pushing and a shoving I can tell you. It take tree of de pall bearers to get Miss Clarissa down from de rostrum.

De priest get so confused, he read de burial rites at de parlour like if he was going to bury Pinkie right dere. Your Granny and me sit down and we ain't move a muscle. We wait till de procession move off and only go as far as de gate of de cemetery. I tell you. We gotta be careful how we live. If yuh live in confusion, yuh gwine dead in confusion." Miss Daisie was out of breath.

Uncle Tom suddenly snapped his fingers, then burst out, "Now I remember where I know her from. She used to live in Providence Village, but her name was not Miss Clarissa but Miss Clarke. The people called her the town crier because she would visit bereaved families who were putting together the burial service and offer her own service to cry at the funeral for a fee."

I gasped, Auntie Gillie sat upright, and Alicia paid close attention. Even Granny Shiela was listening intently.

"It seemed that some families really did pay her to cry at the funerals of their dearly departed, but Miss Clarke lost credibility when she mixed up the names of two women who had died and began her caterwauling at Miss Haynes funeral, saying that she was the best market vendor. The family were not amused since Miss Haynes was a past head teacher. So the people in Providence said they did not want a town crier in their village and made her life a misery until she left. I didn't realise she had ended up here." Uncle Tom shook his head.

"Miss Clarissa was a certified town crier?" I asked.

"A certified lunatic, if you ask me," Alicia stated before leaving the room.

"Golden Grove not ready for dat kind of behaviour," Granny Shiela said. "She needs to stop, or somebody will stop her."

"I better tell de priest and dem to look out for she," Miss Daisie said. "Dis cyant happen again. I going to de eating up dey have after de burial. Alyuh coming?"

"Do not call my name in your reporting please," Uncle Tom warned. He was itching to use the word "gossiping".

"No, we are not," Auntie Gillie answered firmly. "Tom is leaving in de next two days, and we have some packing to complete."

"Oh yes," Miss Daisie said. She got up with haste to go and spread the news, but now she sat back down. "Is where you will be staying. I have two girlfriends and deir daughters living in London. I can give you deir address."

"He's not sure," Granny Shiela said. "Yuh had better run along before de food finish. Yuh know how people like to eat and drink at dese functions."

"Is true." Miss Daisie got up again and left hurriedly.

"Food will do it every time," Granny Shiela said with satisfaction. "Daisie mout does run like when horse ah trot. We business wudda reach far and wide."

The next day Golden Grove was abuzz with the news of Miss Clarke now known as Miss Clarissa. The bad reputation of Miss Clarke, the village crier was had been revealed.

The second interesting event was when Uncle Tom's nephew offered him a birthday trip to England. Uncle Tom thought it was a good opportunity for him to see his youngest sibling whom he had not seen for twenty years. Auntie Gillie was unhappy about the trip even though she knew it was for just six weeks.

"So who is going to put on the gas head when the gas finishes?" she grouched. "How are we going to cook? And who will clean and fill the water tank in preparation for the rainy season?"

There were so many unanswered questions that Granny Shiela got quite cross and snapped at her. "For Christ's sake Gillie. Give de man some breeze. It done seventeen years since yuh all marry and he here at yuh beck and call. Yuh just being selfish!"

Auntie Gillie was so surprised she didn't say another word about the trip. There was a big smile on Uncle Tom's face and although he tried to hide his glee, we could see he was extremely excited. It was the first time he was going on an airplane—and so far away from home.

Granny Shiela pushed up slowly from the chair. "I am going to change dese clothes, bade and take a lie down. Sue, come and help your Granny."

"Are you ill, Granny Shiela?" I asked worriedly.

"No, just tired," she said, and holding on to my arm we left the room.

Two weeks later, Uncle Tom left for his long-anticipated holiday to England and Auntie Gillie looked lost and forlorn until Granny Shiela snapped at her. "Pull yourself together!"

It was a gloomy afternoon and every now and then the sky wept. I sat in the porch and thought about Miss Clarissa. I should have known there was something unnatural about her. I could not understand how was it possible for her to cry—just like that! I looked around carefully before I verbalized, "Crazy, but with kind intentions!"

I had already reasoned it out. Some people felt so frozen during a tragedy, or when a catastrophe occurred they could not cry. There was nothing harmful if someone else cried for them. Was it wrong to employ a crier for a funeral?

Guided Questions

1. Who is the main character in this story?
2. What two themes are highlighted in this story?
3. What is the highest point of a story called?
4. Where did the main event of the story take place?
5. What is the main role of Miss Daisie in this chapter?
6. How does Uncle Tom help the reader to understand Miss Clarissa's behaviour?
7. Auntie Gillie shows another side of her character. Explain what is it.

Discussion

Discuss someone you know who can cry whenever he/she wants to. Why do such persons cry?

Do you think a funeral is an appropriate place to mention the bad experiences in a person's life? Why or why not?

You may have heard a person say "my spirit don't tek he/she" Explain in your own words what this expression means.

Research those countries that use "village criers".

Chapter Twenty

When Life Gives You Lemons...

One of the old women in Golden Grove whom I loved deeply was Miss Lorna Reddington. Granny Shiela said she came from Surinam to work with a Dutch family. When the family decided to relocate to Holland, they left Miss Lorna "high and dry" but she didn't let that dampen her effervescent spirit.

A short, cuddly old woman with a wide mouth, she always had a broad smile on her face and a story to tell. She would throw back her head and laugh loudly. Her uncontrollable laughter was contagious, and passers-by found themselves chuckling even though they hadn't the faintest clue about the joke being shared.

"Yuh must take what Miss Lorna tell you wid a pinch of salt, eh," Granny Shiela said.

"Why, Granny Shiela?" I asked.

"Ah don't know if half de tings she say is true," Granny Shiela responded.

"I still like her," I retorted stubbornly.

One of the most endearing qualities of Miss Lorna was her ability to laugh at herself. I wondered if Granny Shiela was jealous of her.

"She always look as if she has a bad hair day," Alicia remarked. "I don't know if is her own hair—it looks like a wig to me. But if it's not twisted to one side, it needs brushing." She laughed mockingly. Sometimes Alicia could be nice, but at other times, she was so mean.

"I like that woman," Uncle Tom said. "Not many people have a sense of humour, and to reach that age, and still retain her smile, after all the disappointments in life is a testament to the quality of the woman. When I look at her, I think of the statement when life gives you lemons, make lemonade". She is one of a kind."

This is indeed high praise from Uncle Tom, I thought.

"You are right Tom," Auntie Gillie gave an indulgent smile. "Last week, Miss Lorna joined our line dancing group for women my age." Auntie Gillie patted her hair.

Since Uncle Tom returned from England, Auntie Gillie was ever so supportive of whatever he said and did. According to Granny Shiela, "Absence makes de heart grow fonder, indeed."

The energized couple went for dinner once every week and Auntie Gillie began to spruce up her hair, get her nails done, and pay attention to the way she dressed at home. I was quite shocked to see Auntie Gillie pottering around the garden in tights. For goodness sake! Whoever heard of a fifty-something-year-old woman wearing tights? Yeech! Now she had joined line dancing!

"She was the oldest person there." Auntie Gillie gave a girlish giggle before she continued. "When the music started, everybody going to the right, Miss Lorna going to the left. People get so distracted by trying to correct her that the dance instructor stopped and took Miss Lorna to a one-to-one session before we start back. And you know what? She got the hang of it." Auntie Gillie laughed long and hard. "It was a sight to behold, I tell you! Miss Lorna doing line dancing!"

"Lorna needs to move wid people her age," Granny Shiela grumbled. "I'm sure she is in her mid-seventies. What she have to do wid line dancing amongst people in deir 50s and 60s?"

"If that makes her happy, I don't see why it should bother you," Uncle Tom said, looking displeased. "Maybe if you tried it, you might not suffer from high blood pressure, diabetes or complain of pains here and aches there." Uncle Tom got up and left the room. Granny Shiela looked dumbfounded, and Auntie Gillie examined her nails.

I cornered Uncle Tom later that evening when he was outside sneaking a pull from his tobacco pipe.

"Uncle Tom," I called out. "Can I ask you a question?"

Uncle Tom looked around guiltily before he answered. "You have to promise not to tell Gillie you saw me smoking."

"I wouldn't," I said earnestly, "but you have to promise to tell me the truth. Let's shake hands on it." We shook hands solemnly.

"Now Uncle Tom, what did you mean when you said life had given Miss Lorna lemons?"

Uncle Tom look resigned before he responded. "I should have known you would pick up on that. You too smart for your own good." He shook his head.

I inched closer then sat down on a stool that was conveniently placed for when Uncle Tom elevated his leg.

Uncle Tom took a long drag from his pipe then mused, "Where should I begin?"

"At the beginning," I urged.

"You must learn patience, young lady," Uncle Tom admonished. "I have to get my thoughts together."

We sat in silence for a minute. The pungent smoke from the tobacco pipe lingered in the atmosphere as he blew it upwards. He began haltingly, his voice a low rumble.

"You ever notice Miss Lorna always wears a wig?"

"I was wondering 'bout that," I admitted in a shamefaced manner. I didn't want to be as mean as Alicia.

"Yes-s-s," Uncle Tom dragged out the words slowly. "Miss Lorna had a hard life. She grew up in the country area in Surinam and her mother sent her to town to live with one of the well-to-do families. The family migrated to Guyana to live, and they worked her like a dog, I tell you. So the first young man that smiled up with her, she was easily fooled. When she got pregnant, she was terribly ashamed. Back then it was a disgrace to get pregnant and not be married. The oldest girl of the family took the baby and went away to Holland with it. She never saw the child after it was born.

"By age thirty-six, Lorna had six children and none of them ever lived with her," Uncle Tom added. "As far as I know three are in the States, one in

Africa and another one in Spain. I don't know whatever became of the sixth one"

"Who take them, Uncle Tom?" I asked.

"Different friends of her employer. Her employer made Lorna feel as though she was the wickedest young lady ever to have been born."

"That's really sad, Uncle Tom," I said softly, "She must have been real lonely."

"Well, she did get a chance at happiness when she was thirty-eight. She met a young man about her age, and she loved him very much. However, a much younger woman came on the scene, and he forgot he had pledged undying love to Lorna. You see Lorna couldn't make any more children." Uncle Tom stopped the narrative once again, before he resumed. His voice had grown extremely soft. "In her despair, Lorna attempted suicide by lighting herself afire. It was by the grace of God, a friend went to visit at the same time. Screaming for all she was worth, her friend pushed her to the ground and beat the fire out. That was a true friend, I can tell you. She suffered surface burns. Lorna, on the other hand, suffered second degree burns and her hair was scorched off. Since then it has grown back in patches with bald spots here and there. That is why she always wears a wig."

"How horrible!" I was really distressed. I was silent for a while before I asked, "How do you know so much about her life?"

"Because my uncle was the young man who left her for the younger woman," he admitted in sorrow. "Our family was really heartbroken about the way it turned out."

"I think she moves well with the young people," Uncle Tom added, "because she never got a chance to enjoy her own childhood days." He turned to me and shook an admonishing finger. "Enjoy your childhood while you can. Life moves so fast! Before you know it, your childhood is gone, and you become like some of those older people I know who are desperately trying to recapture their youthful years."

Silence reigned once again before Uncle Tom got up walked inside, leaving me to ponder on his parting words.

The next time I saw Miss Lorna she was enthusiastically discussing the newest arrival in the village with Miss Daisie. Mr. Nelson had a job doing the records at the municipal market in the village. He also had two sons and a very young daughter. The girl would attend my high school. I was going to make friends with her and maybe get an introduction to her brothers!

"Mr. Nelson was a teacher before he get promoted to dis job," Miss Lorna told Miss Daisie. "He say he will continue to give evening classes in Physics."

My ears perked up. I was a bit weak in Physics. I would ask Auntie Gillie to investigate further. The weekend swept in without fanfare, and I was on my way to the library to meet my study group when I saw Miss Lorna surrounded by a group of women.

I inched closer. I often collected information about the people I met during the day. It gave rise to spirited discussions during our evening meals.

"You have to be very careful whenever you pass by de Water Works office," Miss Lorna's hand movements always emphasized everything she said.

"What yuh mean Miss Lorna," a young woman asked from the edge of the crowd.

"I hope is not anodder bomb scare prank," Miss Davis said. Her voice was heavy and deep. All eyes were now trained on Miss Lorna's face.

"No," Miss Lorna responded. "Dere is a blackbird nest at de top of de building and de birds dem swooping down and pecking people in deir head. I had to run to get away from dem." I wanted to laugh as I thought of Miss Lorna running.

At this point, the young woman gave a gasp, and burst out laughing before she asked, "But Miss Lorna, where is your wig?"

All eyes fixed on Miss Lorna's head and there it was! Just a knotted piece of black stocking that formed a cap, surrounded by tufts of grey, scruffy hair.

"Oh Lawd," Miss Lorna shouted, patting her head. "De blackbirds an dem peck off me wig." As the crowd of women began to laugh uproariously, Miss Lorna joined in their merriment as comments and advice flew from all directions.

"Maybe de birds dem tink is a bird's nest," one woman remarked. Laugher erupted afresh.

"You gwine haffa retrace yuh steps Miss Lorna. You sure to find it," another said helpfully.

"De people at Water Authority shudda done get rid of dem blackbirds ever since. Let dem buy back yuh wig, Miss Lorna," another woman advised.

"Nah," Miss Lorna said with a chuckle. "Dat wig must be done its time. I have plenty more wigs home. I coming bigger and better wid a new one on Sunday at church."

The group of women laughed good-naturedly before they dispersed. I smiled to myself, *What a woman! Someone else would have been embarrassed for days. Not Miss Lorna!*

I retraced my steps to look for Miss Lorna's wig. It did not matter I would be late for the group work, but the wig was nowhere to be seen. I concluded the blackbirds had indeed taken it to their nests, or the sanitation workers swept the pavement and deposited the wig into the garbage bin. I shrugged. From what she had said, Miss Lorna had a collection of wigs from which she could choose. The incident was sure to be a topic for conversation at the dinner table that evening. I fully understood what Uncle Tom meant when he said, "When life gives you lemons...."

Guided Questions

1. The story takes place in two separate locations. Name them.
2. Identify the different conflicts discussed in this chapter.
3. What is Uncle Tom's connection with Miss Lorna?
4. How did Miss Lorna react to her rejection by the man she loved?
5. How do you think Uncle Tom felt about the way Miss Lorna reacted to her rejection?
6. How has Miss Lorna reacted to all the problems she experienced in life?
7. Why do you think Granny Shiela disliked Miss Lorna?
8. Find a word that can replace the phrase "using hand movements for emphasis".
9. Explain in your own words what the title of this story is saying.
10. You have discussed "imagery" as a figurative device. Identify what you consider as a phrase containing the strongest imagery in this story.

Discussion

Do you agree that Miss Lorna's children should have been taken away from her? Give reasons for your answer.

Is suicide the answer to life's problems? Discuss the alternatives that can be used.

What valuable lesson have you learned from this story?

Why do you think Sue wants an introduction to Mr. Nelson's sons?

How has Sue begun to show changes in her behaviour since the book began?

Find out from your science teacher what can be responsible for the heavy, deep voices of some persons as opposed to high-pitched voices?

Research

Find out which country in the Caribbean has the highest suicide rate. Write a letter for a school magazine condemning suicide as an answer to the problems of life.

Epilogue

I got up from the chair, my knees creaking in protest. The memories receded. I knew they would return. The incidents that shaped my identity would return to play out in my mind, stark and clear as though it was happening, right there and then!

"Yes," I said firmly to myself, ignoring the quivering sound of my voice, "They will return. At least old age hasn't affected my mind."

I looked around guiltily, but no one was there to hear me talking to myself. Three of my four children had moved away from the family home. Derek lived in Canada, while Carol resided in England. Martin was somewhere globe trotting. Every time I heard from him, he was in one country or the other. They only came for a visit at Christmas time to get away from the brutal cold in which they lived. When my husband, Linden, had passed on to the great beyond, Christine and her family had remained with me, and I couldn't ask for a better daughter. She, her husband and her two children, Charmaine and Bradley, made my old age one of contentment, rather than making me feel like a burden.

Footsteps heralded my granddaughter's arrival. "Granny Sue, you want anything to drink? And Ma make split peas soup with pieces of pigtail and corned pork. Your favourite food! The dumplings nice and soft so you won't have to take out your false teeth to eat them."

As I looked at this replica of myself, I smiled. Many days she sat with me and listened as I reminisced. I hope the legacy I leave behind will continue to echo through the ages. I can't wait for the memories to resurface, to embrace those pieces of my past that shaped my identity.

Biographies

Gwenette Pearson Cambridge, Author

Born in Guyana, South America, Gwenette Pearson Cambridge has been an educator for over forty years. She resides in St. Vincent and the Grenadines, having married her Vincentian penfriend. She holds a Bachelor of Education (B.Ed.) in Educational Administration (UWI) and a Master of Science (MSC) with focus on Early Childhood Education. Now retired, Mrs. Pearson Cambridge spends her time writing poetry and books for children and adults. She also tutors students in the complexities of English Language and Literature.

Christine Browne, Illustrator

Christine Browne is a freelance artist and illustrator from St. Vincent and the Grenadines. She holds a Bachelor's degree in Visual Arts from the University of the West Indies, Trinidad. From 2014 to 2018 she taught art at One School Global in St. Vincent, one of a network of independent schools established by the Plymouth Brethren Christian Church. Her illustrations focus on whimsical- themed characters based on the many unique and diverse cultures of people throughout the world. She is expanding her network under her brand name cmdbART.